I Will Glory in the Cross

Pastor Jean Tracey

Note for Librarians: A cataloguing record for this book is available from Library
and Archives Canada at www.collectionscanada.ca/amicus/index-e.html

Printed in Victoria, BC, Canada.

Editor: Daniel Langfried

ISBN: 978-1-4251-9034-7 (Soft)
ISBN: 978-1-4251-9037-8 (e-book)

*We at Trafford believe that it is the responsibility of us all, as both individuals
and corporations, to make choices that are environmentally and socially sound.
You, in turn, are supporting this responsible conduct each time you purchase a
Trafford book, or make use of our publishing services. To find out how you are
helping, please visit www.trafford.com/responsiblepublishing.html*

*Our mission is to efficiently provide the world's finest, most comprehensive
book publishing service, enabling every author to experience success.
To find out how to publish your book, your way, and have it available
worldwide, visit us online at www.trafford.com*

Trafford rev. 6/15/2009

Trafford
PUBLISHING www.trafford.com

North America & international
toll-free: 1 888 232 4444 (USA & Canada)
phone: 250 383 6864 ♦ fax: 250 383 6804 ♦ email: info@trafford.com

The United Kingdom & Europe
phone: +44 (0)1865 487 395 ♦ local rate: 0845 230 9601
facsimile: +44 (0)1865 481 507 ♦ email: info.uk@trafford.com

10 9 8 7 6 5 4 3 2 1

Lord Jesus,

Please anoint me with a supernatural anointing as I write "I Will Glory in the Cross."

Lord, please bless me with the grace and the strength to write this book. I do need divine wisdom, divine knowledge, divine understanding.

Please help me Lord. You will get all the glory, the honor and the praise.

Thank you Lord, in Jesus name.

And he said unto me, My grace is sufficient for thee: for my strength is made perfect in weakness. Most gladly therefore will I rather glory in my infirmities, that the power of Christ may rest upon me. Therefore I take pleasure in infirmities, in reproaches, in necessities, in persecutions, in distresses for Christ's sake: for when I am weak, then am I strong.

2 Corinthians 12:9-10

But God forbid that I should glory, save in the cross of our Lord Jesus Christ, by whom the world is crucified unto me, and I unto the world.

Galatians 6:14

FROM THE AUTHOR,

God had spoken to me about 15 years ago, about this book. He gave me the name of the book when He spoke to me. In July 2008, the Lord said "Jean, start the book." I obeyed Him and I did. God told me that He would use this book to bless many all over the world. This book is to be small so that it will be easy to carry around.

Father God,

I pray for every person that will read this book, that the Holy Spirit will quicken your people. I pray, God, that you will bless your people with spiritual wisdom, knowledge and understanding, and that your people would want to serve God in spirit and in truth.

I pray Lord that no matter what your people are called to go through in life, they would be willing, because you give them the grace and the strength.

Lord, you are no respecter of persons. Bless your people Lord as they read this book,

In Jesus' name,

Amen

From the Editor,

Glimpses of God are seen throughout this book as senior Pastor Jean Tracey describes her many remarkable, life changing encounters with the Living God and Saviour.

Through trials, tribulation and endurance she has repeatedly sought to persevere and overcome as she has fought the enemy and interceded for many souls.

It is my prayer that this work will increase your faith, encourage your heart to seek a more intimate relationship with God, and compel you to live a life Holy and pleasing to Him in every way. Make sure you put on the full armor of God (see Ephesians 6:11) before reading.

Yours in Christ Jesus,
Daniel

But without faith it is impossible to please him: for he that cometh to God must believe that he is, and that he is a rewarder of them that diligently seek him.

Hebrews 11:6

My Childhood Days

I was born in Guyana, South America on a little Island called Leguan. Guyana is divided into three counties; Essequibo, Demerara and Berbice. Leguan is in the Essequibo River. I had five brothers and five sisters. One of my brothers died by accident when I was in my early teens. I have four living brothers and five sisters. Out of the ten, I am number seven. We were very poor; we lived in a little house with two bedrooms, a little living room, and a little kitchen. We didn't have many clothes and we didn't have luxuries. We had no refrigerator or stove, just a few chairs and a little table and two little beds. We used to cook on what we called a fireside, which is made with mud. To make a fire, you had to arrange the wood in the fireside, then throw a little kerosene oil on the wood, and light it with matches.

Though we were very poor, we always had plenty to eat. We never went hungry. My mom and dad always made sure there was food, and they bought food in bulk. I think my father was a gardener. My mother used to work very hard in the rice fields, cutting rice. My brothers worked very hard to help my mother support us.

Though we were very poor, we grew up in a home filled with love. My mother always took care of us very well. She cooked all the time, baked bread, and made nice goodies for us, cakes, etc. My father was a very religious man, and he was a very strict father. I was his pet. He used to put me on his shoulders and walk me to school when I was very young. My father died when I was about eight years old. Amazingly, I remember a lot about my father. Oh I missed him so much, I used to cry everyday for him. Even now, I can describe my father to anybody.

I remembered seeing my father reading his Bible all the time – he was an Anglican. We had a little veranda and he would put out his rocking chair, and he would put his feet on the rail and read his Bible. At times he whistled old, Anglican hymns. I do not know if my father went to Heaven, because although my dad was religious, he did many wrong things. He was in adultery, and he used to beat up my mother. I never witnessed these events, but my mother told me about them. I knew a lot about him, because when I grew up I asked my mother a lot of questions. I do hope he went to Heaven because I really loved both my parents. We had a huge piece of land, but our house was tiny. We also had many fruit trees. At the front of our little house my father always planted very beautiful and colorful flowers. I think he was a gardener.

THE STAR-APPLE
TREE

God's hand was upon me since I was a child. When I was five or six years old, I came home from school to have my lunch. My father fetched me from school on his shoulders, and my parents washed my hands and I sat down by the kitchen steps eating with my hands. The kitchen steps were at the back of the house then. Years later, my mother renovated the kitchen and put the steps at the front of the house.

While I was eating by the kitchen steps at the back of the house, something amazing happened. We had a huge star-apple tree not far from where I was eating. I was sitting there all by myself, enjoying my food, and my parents were inside the house. As I was eating, a very strong wind began blowing on me. Now, I know for a fact it had to be God that, in that very hour, not only gave me a visitation, He also gave me divine wisdom to check things out. The wind was blowing so strongly on me. It was as if a huge fan was blowing on me at its highest speed. This is the only way I can describe it. We didn't have a fan. We didn't even have electricity on that little island in those days. The wisdom God gave me in that hour is amazing. At that age, where would I get that sense to check out the trees? God is awesome. I looked at the branches of the trees to see if they were shaking, and everything was very still. It wasn't a storm, and it wasn't windy. I looked and looked and there was no indication of even a little bit of wind. It was lunch time and the sun was so hot. It was very bright and clear out. There was a star-apple tree very close by to where I was eating. There were other fruit trees all around, but the star-apple tree was my focus.

As the Lord lives, this is what took place: while I was eating, the wind that was blowing on me took me up in the air. As I looked around, I saw I was in line with the top of the very tall star-apple tree. I was off the ground pretty high. In that hour, God gave me wisdom. I was even checking out the top of the star-apple tree, and lining myself with the top of it. God is very real. I did not scream and I wasn't crying; I was very calm. Then the same wind that took me up brought me back right down to the exact spot where my plate and cup were. I came back down safely, no hurt, nothing, everything was normal again. Then I got up, took my plate and my cup into the kitchen, and I called my parents. I took them by the kitchen steps where I was eating, and told them exactly what had happened. They listened to me very intently, but they had nothing to say. Finally, my dad said "Get ready, I will take you to school." He quickly put me on his shoulders, and he took me to school.

This experience I will never forget as long as I live. Sometimes I sit and ponder the whole scene. I was never afraid going up, nor coming down - I had perfect peace. This event will always be a part of me; it is like it happened yesterday. On August 14th, 2008 I turned sixty years old, and I do remember everything.

Psalm 118:16-17 The right hand of the LORD is exalted: the right hand of the LORD doeth valiantly. I shall not die, but live, and declare the works of the LORD.

Tender Care

My dad died when I was about eight years old. Even from that age, I can remember growing up with so much love for people, especially older folks, and the little children like myself. There was an elderly lady who was our neighbor, and she was nearly always at our home. We gave her food everyday and she was very close to my mother. When she got sick, I would help her out. I would bring her food, help her sweep her house, help her wash dishes – you name it.

Our other neighbor was also very old and sickly. He was taking care of his two grandchildren because they didn't have parents. I think both of their parents died. They were extremely poor. Though we were very poor, we always had plenty of food. Stealing my mother's rice and flour and sugar potatoes, I would give them to this old man to cook for himself and his two grandchildren. My mother used to give us a shilling every Saturday afternoon to buy ice cream. My sisters and brothers would buy their ice cream. I would take my shilling (today you call it a quarter) and I would go to the fence, call him over and give him the shilling, and I would go without my cone. I had such joy doing it. Only God could have given me that joy. God was teaching me to love in deed and truth. God granted me compassion.

1 John 3:17-18 But whoso hath this world's good, and seeth his brother have need, and shutteth up his bowels of compassion from him, how dwelleth the love of God in him? My little children, let us not love in word, neither in tongue; but in deed and in truth.

That man would take that money, and he would say "My daughter, God Bless you." Then he would go to the store and buy 12 loaves for a shilling. One loaf in those days cost a penny. Their family would have it on Sunday morning and Sunday night for dinner.

Matthew 6:20 But lay up for yourselves treasures in heaven, where neither moth nor rust doth corrupt, and where thieves do not break through nor steal:

He had two grandchildren; one boy and one girl. They were younger than I. I was 12 years old at the time, the girl was six, and the boy was four. Lice were crawling all over their heads. When my mother went to the rice fields, I would take care of the two children. We had a neighbor that had a stand pipe in their yard. I would go there and give them a good scrub down. My mom had a spray for mosquitoes called DDT. Before I bathed them, I would spray their heads with this stuff, and I would tie up their hair in a towel and let it sit for one hour, then untie it and most of the lice would die. Then I would put them under this stand pipe and give them a bath, and I would wash their hair thoroughly and give them clean clothes to put on. Next, I would cook and give them something to eat. My mother had taught me to cook from the age of 10.

Afterwards I started to take care of the children in the village. Taking three bricks, I would set them up with wood, light the fire, take my mother's pots, and cook rice and stew for all the children. I cooked lots of food for them. I would give them all a bath and clean clothes - old things my mother washed and put away in boxes. I would take them out and give them to the kids. I would go to the neighbors and beg them not to say anything to my mother when she got home from work, since my mother always warned us about playing with fire.

I did this kind of thing until I was thirteen or fourteen years old. I also used to ask my sisters and brothers not to tell on me. Everyone was very cooperative. Since we always had plenty of food (because we bought food in bulk), my mother did not miss anything when I took it to cook for the children. It had to be God that gave me the love and compassion for those older people and for those little children who were hungry. They were not just fed. They had a good bath and clean clothes – this had to be God. I used to wash up all the dishes and clean the pots and everything, dry them, and put them back in their right places before my mother came home. No neighbors, nor my brothers and sisters told on me – no one.

Romans 8:28 And we know that all things work together for good to them that love God, to them who are the called according to his purpose.

My Teen Years

My mother taught all her girls to cook from an early age. We had to, we didn't have a choice. We cooked, we learned to bake, and we learned to do housework from an early age. At school I was very athletic. Oh, and I loved it. I used to play on the girl's cricket team and was a wicket keeper. I was very involved at school. My school mates and I used to clean the Anglican Church which was right at the front of our school. We cleaned the church every Friday afternoon after school. School was great; I had good teachers, and I was well liked. My mother taught us a lot about respect for people. At age 15 or 16 I had to quit school when my older sister got married because I had to take charge of everything in the house; the cooking, cleaning, baking and everything else. My mother had to work in the rice fields; therefore I had no other choice. So I did what I had to do gracefully in every way I could. I was still going to the Anglican Church, and so forth.

1 Corinthians 15:10 But by the grace of God I am what I am: and his grace which was bestowed upon me was not in vain; but I laboured more abundantly than they all: yet not I, but the grace of God which was with me.

Marriage

A few guys came home to my mother, to ask if they could marry me. I didn't like any of them. And when my future husband came, my mother liked him. I had great respect for my mother. She said: "Jean, I am getting old now, and I would like you to get married before I die." I said "Yes ma, whatever you say, I will do." No dating of course. That was a no no. So I got married when I was 18 years old. I designed my own wedding dress. I told the seamstress exactly what I wanted. My wedding and everything went well. My husband was from Bartica, Guyana, in South America.

Ephesians 6:1 Children, obey your parents in the Lord: for this is right.

My husband used to work at a place called Winneperu, 30 miles from Bartica. He was a driver and he used to drive a low bed (at least that is what they called it). He named it Jean. We lived at Winneperu for a while, and I became pregnant with my first child.

The Accident

O ne day my husband went to work with my uncle. My uncle lived at Winneperu with my aunt and their children, and worked for the same company my husband worked for. The two of them went out to work together that day and as they sat together in the low bed driving, they were making a turn, and they had an accident. There were two valleys; one on the right side, and one on the left. When the accident occurred my husband jumped from the vehicle in the valley, and my uncle jumped from the vehicle into the other valley. Tragically, my uncle died.

When the news came to me saying that one died and they didn't know which one, I thought it was my husband. I started to scream. I was about 5 months pregnant, and the baby leaped in my womb for the first time. Then they brought my husband home. It was quite an overwhelming experience. At Winneperu there was no church to attend, so after I got married I stopped going to church. However, I would still read my Bible everyday. Even though I was sad about my uncle's death, I went on my knees, and I thanked God for sparing my husband's life.

1 Thessalonians 5:18 In every thing give thanks: for this is the will of God in Christ Jesus concerning you.

This occurred about four months before my first child was born. It was a custom in those days to go to your mother's house and have your baby there. I did go home to my mother, approximately when I entered nine months. My mother took such good care of me, and all her children. To me she was the best mother in the whole wide world. On the little island where my mother lived and where I grew up there was a midwife, a very old woman, who was very skilled when it came to her job. She was very knowledgeable and experienced; my mother and her were good friends for many years. While I was at my mother's home leading up to the end of the pregnancy, she would come to visit me just to see how I was doing. She was deaf, and in order to communicate with her one would have to speak loudly. She was a nice woman, but she was very serious. She would give you a smile sparingly. When she came to visit, she would sit and have breakfast with us, and we would chat for a while.

My First Child

Soon, my first child would be born. I woke up in the morning very early as I always did. I had my bath, and I started to comb my hair. I felt a pain as no other pain in my whole life. I ran to my mother, we called her ma. All her children called her ma. "Ma, I have a lot of pain." I said. She sent for the nurse right away, and the nurse came. I was in labor for many hours. When the baby did come, I was unconscious for about half an hour or a little longer. When I opened my eyes the place was filled with people, inside the house and outside - packed with people. I said to my mother: "Ma, what are all these people here for and why is everyone crying?" She replied "We thought you died, and we were screaming, so all the neighbors ran over, and other people heard and they all came." I had an extremely difficult delivery.

Genesis 3:16 Unto the woman he said, I will greatly multiply thy sorrow and thy conception; in sorrow thou shalt bring forth children; and thy desire shall be to thy husband, and he shall rule over thee.

Thank God that woman knew her job well. I wasn't in the church since I got married, but I prayed and read my Bible everyday, the best I knew how. Although I wasn't in church, God never gave up on me. I know for a fact it had to be God that brought me through safely. My first son was born - Gary Tracey. He weighed 15 lbs. Now you see why I nearly died. When they gave the baby a bath and they got him dressed and put him on the bed he looked like a three month old baby.

Because it was my first child, I didn't know too much, so I ate and drank any and everything, and it wasn't the best for me. I drank a lot of coke, and I loved a lot of ice. You name it, I had it. The baby was huge, but God saw me through. My mother took very good care of me and my baby. I stayed there for a while until I was strong enough to go back to my husband, and he would come to visit us while I was at my mom's.

A Stranger at Night

Then my husband went to work at Mackenzie; he got a job with a well paying salary with Guyba, a bauxite company. He was a dragline operator (a very huge machine). His coworkers were very racially prejudiced on the job. They didn't like him and he knew his work well, so they envied him. There were just a few that liked him. He always would tell me that if he got a chance to go overseas, he would go, or if I got a break before him, he would let me go and later he would follow. We used to live across the river at a place called Wismar, so from Mackenzie you took a little boat and crossed the river, and within minutes you arrived at Wismar. We used to rent a very huge house there. One week, it was a Christmas week, my husband was working nights.

One particular night he did not go to work because he wasn't feeling well, and someone broke in. I believe this was someone who knew my husband was working nights, and watched for an opportunity. He must have thought my husband went to work and he came in through a window. Strangely he did not steal anything. I heard a lot about break-ins in the area, and usually they stole a lot, so I never let my kids sleep by themselves. They used to sleep with us in our room.

My eyes opened around 2am in the morning, and I saw a man over me wrapped in a white towel. He looked like a person that had just come out of the shower the way he dressed. I did not scream because I did not want to alarm the children, they were all sound asleep. My husband was sleeping. I tried to wake him up by shaking him with my right hand, and the thief ran out of the house. By the time my husband woke up, the thief ran away, going through the same window he came in. But all of us were safe; he never hurt anyone of us. We saw his footprints and everything on the floor. I don't think he came to steal, because everything was in place; he took nothing. I think he came in to rape me because he thought my husband went to work that night, but my husband wasn't feeling well.

Looking back, this had to be God's hand on my life. Though I wasn't in Church, though I wasn't serving the Lord, He was watching over me, and over my family. I went on my knees and I said "God thank you for protecting us." This is what I would always do; pray for a few minutes every day and ask God's protection over us.

Psalm 5:11 But let all those that put their trust in thee rejoice: let them ever shout for joy, because thou defendest them: let them also that love thy name be joyful in thee

A Decision to Move on

Shaken by the break in, I said to my husband "We have to move out of this house and I will try to go overseas. I will try and go to Canada." When we moved to Mackenzie a number of things happened. My children were very small. I was in adultery. I used to drink occasionally. I never liked smoking, so I never smoked. There were lots of ups and downs in our marriage. My husband was a heavy smoker, and he used to drink. He used to beat me once in a while. I can remember he kicked me when I was pregnant with my second child in my stomach. We separated, then we made up back again, and this went on and on. I take a lot of the blame for a lot of the things we went through in the marriage.

Proverbs 17:1 Better is a dry morsel, and quietness therewith, than an house full of sacrifices with strife.

Then I decided to start work on my papers to come to Canada. I began to get my passport and different things in place so I could leave Guyana. I have three children born in Guyana, and one was born in Canada. Gary was six years old then, Bruce was four years old and Gail was about three years old. I had a very good friend in Guyana, and we were very close. She would come to my home and eat whatever she wanted - we lived just like family. I could go to her house and do the same. My friend said to me, "I am going to Canada. I have a daughter over there and I am going for a vacation, maybe you can come along with me, and you can stay at my daughter's place for a little while, and then take it from there." I had cousins in Canada but I didn't know which part of Canada they lived in. So I decided to take up my friend's offer. I didn't know her daughter in Canada, I never met her.

I told my husband everything (we were on very good terms then). I asked him to think about it very carefully. I told him when I go I would try and make the way for him and the children to follow. I said to him "This will not come overnight, it will take some time." After a while he said "You can go." I love my three children, more than my own life. This was really a tough decision. I had a good talk with my mother, who was a very loving and kind hearted woman. I said: "Ma, I will be going to Canada, and I am asking you to please take care of my three children." My mother said yes, she would take care of them. My mother lived in the same house I grew up in, and where my two sons were born. She still lived on that little island of Leguan.

So my children had to go and stay by my mother's in Leguan. I got everything in order and I took my children to my mother. My husband said he would visit the children very often. He said he would give my mother more than enough money to take care of the children and told me I must not worry. He said he would take good care of them and make sure they had everything. I knew once my children were with my mother that she would feed them well and keep them very clean. My good friend that I was going to Canada with arranged the date. I got ready, bought my ticket, and I cried non stop for my children. My friend and I left Guyana in 1973. I missed my husband, my mother and my children so much I cannot put it into words. We landed and we were picked up from the airport, and we went to my friend's daughter's house to stay with her.

Psalm 18:32 It is God that girdeth me with strength, and maketh my way perfect.

LIFE IN CANADA

When I arrived at my friend's daughter's house from the airport, I asked the daughter if she would allow me to have a shower. She said yes. She gave her mother her dinner, and she gave her coffee. She didn't offer me anything to eat, or drink. After my shower, she took me down in her basement and she said, "Here is where you will sleep." She gave me no covers, no blanket, nothing. She put me on an old sofa to sleep on. Then she and her husband went off to bed.

When my friend saw they went to bed, she came downstairs and gave me her supper. But I could not eat. I told my friend I have no appetite. So I asked her to eat her food. She brought the kettle downstairs and she made some coffee for me. She started to cry, and would not stop apologizing. She said "Jean when I used to visit your home in Guyana I could eat and drink whatever I wanted. Now you are at my daughter's house, and she has not offered you a piece of bread." I said to her "Please do not worry, I am fine." But I wasn't fine. I was in shock. I said to my friend "You go up to your room, you must be really tired" and she went.

I cried all night and I did not sleep. My friend came down and had given me something from her bed to cover with.

Psalm 34:18 The LORD is nigh unto them that are of a broken heart; and saveth such as be of a contrite spirit.

A New Day

Morning came and when the husband and wife of the house went to work, I got up and I took a shower. I got dressed, and went and pulled the drapes in the living room, and looked out to see what the road was like with all the buses running up and down. My friend woke up and made me some coffee, and asked me if I would like some toast. I replied "No thank you." (I was wondering if maybe her daughter had counted the slices of her bread before she left). I didn't want to get my friend in trouble so I refused nicely; "I am not hungry." But trust me, I was very hungry. I drank the coffee my friend gave me.

After my friend went to the washroom, I went out the front door - I didn't have a dime on me. In those days you could not leave Guyana with any money. I saw a newspaper called 'The Toronto Star.' I read the name while I was standing there. When I went out the door, I saw a bus stop right in front of the house. At this bus stop was a line up. A few steps down from this bus stop was a newspaper box. I decided to go to the back of the line to ask an old man for some money. I didn't want to go to anybody young. I was about 26 years old. I said "Sir, I need to buy a newspaper, but I don't have any change this time. I don't have a dime." The man replied "That is ok, I have lots of change, here is a quarter, go get yourself a newspaper." He called the coin he gave me a quarter. I didn't know anything about Canadian money - I just arrived. I responded "Thank you sir, and God Bless you." I don't know how it came out, but it did. I said it. I read the instructions on how to open the machine, put in the quarter and bought the newspaper. It was around 9 or 10 o'clock in the morning.

I ran back into the house with the newspaper. I sat my friend down, and I said to her "This is my plan. I will now look for a job in this newspaper, and if I get one I would like you to know I am leaving." I told her not to try and stop me. She replied "But you just arrived yesterday, you can't go right now. Why don't you rest up for a few days?" I replied, "I can't."

I got out the classified section of the newspaper and I went in the basement where there was a phone. I took out a pen from my handbag and I went through the ad for housekeepers. I had ticked off with my pen about 6 positions. The very first call I made the woman was very nice on the phone. Remember I wasn't saved then, so I used to tell a lot of lies. I told her my name and everything. I told her I have experience with three children. Then she said "You sound like the person I am looking for. Would you be able to come for an interview right now? I have to go to my office in a while, if you take a bus it will take too long." She said to me "Call a taxi right away." I told her I didn't have any money, because I wasn't working for a while. She said "Don't worry, you come, I will let the cab wait for you and I will pay the whole thing." "Thank you Madam, that is very kind of you," I replied.

On the woman's refrigerator, there were cab numbers, about three of them, one called Beck's taxis. They took me right to the woman's door, because I had written down her address.

We introduced ourselves, and she introduced two lovely little children to me. She saw the children took a liking to me right away, and she was very pleased with that. The children were not hers, she adopted both of them. When she asked me how long I lived in Canada I said 6 months. She asked me other questions; I answered all of them, telling lies and more lies. She said she would pay me $40 a week, one hundred and sixty dollars a month. She said it is a live in job, and she asked me if that was ok. I said "That is what I am looking for." She was a lawyer, and her husband was also.

They were Jewish, and she had a lovely home. She showed me to my room, it was beautiful. It had a television and everything in it. Then she requested I go back with the same taxi, and bring some clothes, pack up a suitcase and come back with the same cab. She said she would go and talk to the cab driver who was waiting for me outside. She went and spoke to him. She told him "This lady will start to work with me today. I would kindly ask you to take her back home, wait for her, until she packs up her suitcase, and then bring her right back to my home. I will pay all of it, plus I will tip you real well."

The guy did exactly what he was told. My suitcase was the same way I left it since I landed the day before. All I had to add was what I had slept with, plus my towel plus a few other things, little things. I pushed these on top, and locked my suitcase. I told my friend "Thanks for everything, I got the job and I have to go because the taxi is waiting on me. I will call you on the phone to explain everything." She said,

"But you don't have any money, who will pay the taxi?" "The woman who just employed me," I replied. She was going to give me some pocket money, because she said her daughter had given her some, but I refused, "No thank you, I will be fine." She was really crying and she never stopped apologizing. I said, "Don't worry, things will work out." Then I kissed her goodbye and I left.

When I got there, I rang the doorbell and she came out to pay the cab driver and she took me in with a big hug. Then she gave me lunch and I ate with her and the kids at the same table. She said that after lunch she would go to the office for a couple of hours, and she would be back to prepare dinner and so forth. She said her husband was at the office, because up to that point I had not met him. She told me the kids had to take a nap. She showed me where their snacks were, and what to give them. She said to me "Eat and drink whatever you wish and make yourself comfortable." I did what I had to do. I cleaned up her kitchen and I unpacked my clothes, hung up what I had to, and packed away things in drawers. I washed things, and I bathed her two children (I call them her kids although she adopted them).

Colossians 3:17 And whatsoever ye do in word or deed, do all in the name of the Lord Jesus, giving thanks to God and the Father by him.

The husband and wife were older people. They loved their kids dearly, but spoiled them rotten. There was one boy and one girl. After a while, the couple came in from the office. I met her husband, and he was also very pleasant. He helped her prepare dinner, and they called me to have dinner with them at the same table. When we finished dinner I washed up the dishes, cleaned the kitchen up, and I said goodnight to them all, and took a shower. Then I got on my knees, said my prayers as I always did, and I thanked God for all the miracles he wrought in my life in just one day. I read my Bible for a little while like I always did, even though I wasn't saved. Then I started to weep because I missed all my children, my husband, and my mother so much. After a good long cry I went off to sleep. I worked constantly and very diligently. I did everything; cook, clean, wash and iron. I would iron clothes until midnight, and she would never say "Jean, go to bed now it is late." Never, ever.

When I first had flown to Canada, immigration had given me 3 months to stay. After working for 1 month, I sat her down and I told her the truth about my situation and what had happened. I said to her, "I don't want any last minute confusion. I must respect the immigration rules and their laws." She said, "Ok Jean, I really like you. I will take you in to immigration for a working permit, and I will ask them for an extension." Within a couple of days, she took me in. This was ahead of time, and they gave me a work permit and they stamped my passport. They gave me a one year extension. Praise God.

Genesis 6:8 But Noah found grace in the eyes of the LORD.

Surrender

While I continued to work with this family, I would watch all the religious programs on television. One Sunday I turned on the television and Dr. Oral Roberts came on. The message he was preaching on was entitled "The Fourth Man." It was from the book of Daniel in the Bible, and he was speaking about the three Hebrew children. It was indeed very powerful. I listened very carefully to every word. I never heard anything like it before in my life. I sat on the carpet in front of that television set, and I broke down in tears. He said "Only Jesus can help you, why don't you surrender to Jesus now? If you would like to invite Jesus in your heart, repeat after me this prayer." He said the sinner's prayer and I invited Jesus into my heart.

As I am writing these words, I am going to be 60 years old in two weeks. I was born on the 14th of August, 1948 and I can say 35 years ago I accepted Jesus as my Lord and Saviour and since then, I have never been the same. I love Jesus today more than 35 years ago. Every day he becomes sweeter, and sweeter. I can remember in that little room when I accepted Jesus that day, there was such a peace that came into my life. That very day I asked the Lord for 3 things - I was talking to God in the evening of that very day. I said "God, I need your grace day by day to see me through. I need your divine wisdom day by day to see me through. Lord I want my life to be an open book so that Jesus can be glorified."

Matthew 7:7-8 Ask, and it shall be given you; seek, and ye shall find; knock, and it shall be opened unto you: For every one that asketh receiveth; and he that seeketh findeth; and to him that knocketh it shall be opened.

I know beyond a shadow of a doubt that it was not me praying. It was His precious Holy Spirit. I just accepted Jesus earlier that day. And in a few hours I asked God for these three things. God is so good. He is an awesome God.

Zechariah 4:6 Then he answered and spake unto me, saying, This is the word of the LORD unto Zerubbabel, saying, Not by might, nor by power, but by my spirit, saith the LORD of hosts.

When the Spirit of the Lord led me to pray for those three things, I could have felt it in my bones. I now purposed in my heart to study the word, and pray every day. I did this all my life. Pray for a few minutes every day and read a chapter in the Bible every day. However, now it would not be routine. It would be so different now; a time of joy. Now I am born again and I have the Holy Spirit who is completely in charge. No more boring repetitious prayer. When I go to the word, I will not have the letter.

2 Corinthians 3:6 Who also hath made us able ministers of the new testament; not of the letter, but of the spirit: for the letter killeth, but the spirit giveth life.

I find when I study and pray I have such peace, joy and such strength. It is beyond words.

As I continued to work with this family it got more and more difficult and the biggest problem was with the children. The girl would kick me if I tried to correct her, then her and her brother would spit on me. Now I really see why God saved me in that home; I needed the grace day by day to cope. My boss would take advantage of me because I was quiet and I didn't say anything. They were very nice people, but I worked like a slave and she never raised my salary. Forty dollars a week and that's it. I would stay in from Sunday to Sunday, I had no one to call me, to pick me up to go for fresh air. I felt imprisoned. I couldn't travel to go anywhere because I didn't know how to travel. One day I had a good talk with my boss. I said to her "I need my weekends and I will learn to travel." So I started to travel on the buses, and the subway in all directions. I thank God for the Holy Spirit. He leads, He guides, and He teaches.

John 16:13 Howbeit when he, the Spirit of truth, is come, he will guide you into all truth: for he shall not speak of himself; but whatsoever he shall hear, that shall he speak: and he will shew you things to come.

Now that I started to learn to travel, I would meet people on the buses, and on the trains. I would take phone numbers, of course as the Spirit would have me. I never gave out my boss' phone number. One day I met with a Christian woman, and she invited me to church. I was so happy because it was an answer to prayer; I was praying about a church. Church is very important. Faith will increase as you hear God's word.

Romans 10:17 So then faith cometh by hearing and hearing by the word of God.

I never wanted to miss church as long as I started, this meant a lot to me. I got the directions and I started to go to church every Sunday. For me church was like a school, you learn so much. It was a Pentecostal church and it was ok. I was very eager to know about God, and the Trinity. I wanted to feel God's presence and God's anointing on my life. I was a brand new Christian, a little babe in Christ. Everything the preacher said from the pulpit, I would verify in my room where I stayed on the job. At nights after my shower, I would make sure every thing the Pastor said in church lined up with the word of God. If there is something I didn't understand, I would call up my friend and ask questions; I was so hungry and thirsty for God. On the job I don't get much time. When any little chance came up, I got on my knees and prayed, and I would get in the word any spare minute.

Psalm 42:1 As the hart panteth after the water brooks, so panteth my soul after thee, O God.

By now I had finished about six months on the job and I had an incident with the little girl. One afternoon it started to drizzle and both kids were outside playing with their friends. I went outside and called both of them in, but the girl refused to come in. I got on the phone and I called the boss, and I told her "The rain is falling but the girl would not come in." The boss knew these two children well. They just didn't listen to her, her husband or to me. The little boy would listen to me at times. So she said "Jean I will be home soon." Their office was not far from where they lived. Thank God for that. So I went back outside and I told the little girl "Your mother said she is coming home, so you better get inside quickly." She came to me and she kicked me, and then she spat on me. I started to really cry, and I said "God, that's it, I can't take any more of this. I am going to leave."

When the boss came in, she saw me crying, and she asked me what was wrong. I told her everything and I told her "I am sorry I can't take it anymore, I am leaving." She took me in her bedroom, and she sat me down in her rocking chair, and she went on her knees and began pleading with me. She said "Jean, I will never find someone like you again, no not ever." I said "You are so right, no one will put up with this." I wanted to tell her that no one will iron clothes until midnight for $40 a week, but I didn't say anything. She cried and begged on her knees. I said to her "Your daughter did this many times – this is not the first time. And if this happens one more time I am leaving." The girl was about 4 years old, and the boy was about 3 years old. I have never, under this sun, seen two children spoiled like these two kids. They had absolutely no training whatsoever.

Proverbs 22:15 Foolishness is bound in the heart of a child; but the rod of correction shall drive it far from him.

Now I love children. I just love kids and I do love these two children just like my own, especially the little boy. Both of them were very cute. I thought 'Let me say yes, I will stay, and give it one more chance.' When I told the boss I would stay, she stopped crying immediately. She said "Jean, I thank you." Only God alone knows if she did talk to the child or not. But I was so upset. I went into my room, I prayed and I studied the word, I forgave the child and I moved on.

Matthew 6:14-16 For if ye forgive men their trespasses, your heavenly Father will also forgive you: But if ye forgive not men their trespasses, neither will your Father forgive your trespasses.

Shocking News

My mother and I would have certain days when I would call her to find out how my kids were doing. She didn't have a telephone, so she would have to travel to my aunts' place on the coast once a month, at a place on the coast called Catrina, at Leonora. My mother would go there once a month and I would go to talk with her. There are times I would ask my mom to take the kids, and I would get to talk with them also. My mother told me whenever my husband would visit the children he was always drunk. He was a very heavy drinker.

Proverbs 20:1 Wine is a mocker, strong drink is raging: and whosoever is deceived thereby is not wise.

She said "He doesn't send money often for the children," and many times, he would promise them that he would come to see them, and they would go to meet him at the wharf, and they waited, and he never showed up. The kids were so disappointed they would cry. My mother told me that he had another woman staying with him, that he lived at home with her at Mackenzie, and he wanted all three of the children back. She told me this had been going on for a while now, but she didn't want to say anything to me to make me upset.

If I didn't send money home every month, she said she didn't know what she would do. Every single month from the time I started to work, I faithfully sent money home every month for my mom to buy food for the kids. Because my mom was not working, she took care of my children. I would take out my tithe when I got paid and I used to send $100 a month. My mother had a lot to say on the phone about my husband, and I listened carefully. She was really crying and she apologized for not telling me before. I didn't say too much, but just listened. I was crying on the phone, but I tried my best to restrain myself. So I thanked my mother, and I told her I really wanted to talk to all the children, and asked if she would bring them the next Saturday to my aunt's house. She said yes. I replied, "Goodbye, ma, I love you. Tell the kids I love them, and I will talk to them next week." When I got off the phone, I cried as if there was a funeral. Oh how I love my children, and my mother. I tried to pray and study the word and I cried myself to sleep. God is always so good to me. I thank God for his son Jesus.

1 Peter 5:7 Casting all your care upon him; for he careth for you.

Sure enough, my mother was there with my kids the next Saturday. I spoke to all the children and they were crying, I begged them not to cry. At that time I started to pack a barrel for them, and I told them there will be lots of toys and lots of goodies in the barrel for them, and that I was sending nice clothes for them. I told them to behave themselves. I told them to pray every night before they went to bed, how they must pray, to pray that God would change their dad, and God would help him to stop drinking. I told them to pray and ask God to bring them to Canada soon to be with me, and to pray that God would bless their grandmother with strength and grace everyday. I told the eldest one to write down what I said, and teach the other two also. I spoke to my Ma. I told her "Thanks a lot for taking care of my kids." I told my ma not to worry about anything.

Matthew 6:25 Therefore I say unto you, Take no thought for your life, what ye shall eat, or what ye shall drink; nor yet for your body, what ye shall put on. Is not the life more than meat, and the body than raiment?

I began to really cry out to God in fasting and prayer. I was asking God to save my husband's soul and really deliver him from the spirit of alcohol. The situation got worse.

My husband went to my mother's house and demanded the children from her. She didn't want to give him the children so he went to the police station to report it. When the police came he said that the children were my husband's and my mother was only grandmother, so she had to give him the children. He took them to the woman he lived at home with; so the kids were there with them. This was the worst thing he could have done. When it comes to my kids, I don't fool around. I continued to pray.

Luke 18:1 And he spake a parable unto them to this end, that men ought always to pray, and not to faint;

In my ninth month where I was working, the girl I had the problem with started again with the spitting and the kicking. I had another talk with this child's mother, and she did the same thing, took me to her bedroom and put me in her rocking chair. She kneeled down and begged me for another chance, and she was really crying just like the first time, so I said ok.

About 2 weeks from that day, the whole family went to Germany for two weeks holiday. I thought to myself "Here is my chance." I knew in my heart this was not very Christ like, and 2 days after they were gone, I packed up my stuff and I wrote a note to her, and I said, "I am sorry I have to do it this way, but I don't want to face that same situation a third time." I put the note with her key on the table. In the note I said many thanks for all the things she had done, and when I left there I went to stay with a friend of mine who was very kind to me. She was also a Christian.

In early 1974, I started to prepare to go home to Guyana for a visit. I really wanted to see my children. Oh I missed them so much.

A Journey Home

I told my mom on the phone I was coming home to visit, but I planned to return to Canada. I also asked my mom not to say anything to anyone. My mom was very happy to hear it. I stayed with my mom a few days after I landed, and then I went to Mackenzie, where my husband lived with this woman and my children. I also had two sisters living at Mackenzie; Enid and Elsie. I stayed at Elsie's home. My sister knew a lot about all that was going on with my husband, because he would visit my sister and her family very often. I said to my sister, "Please send for and call my husband because I really would like to see my children before the day is done." So she did - I think it was his day off, so he came right away. When he came to my sister's house, we chatted for a little while, and then I said to him "I would like to see the children, would it be ok if you took me?" He said it was Fine so we took a taxi and we went.

I must admit my husband loves me a lot, and it has always been that way. Somehow I knew in my heart he felt bad about what he was doing. So when we got to the house, the children were very happy to see me. They had on old t-shirts, long ones very old and shabby. They were very thin also. I swallowed all my tears for their sakes, because I didn't want to cry. I met the woman. I greeted her and she was pregnant with my husband's child. I made sure Christ was seen in me from the beginning to the end. I took my kids on my knees, and I hugged them. I prayed with them, and I thanked God for them, and for allowing me to be with them again. I thanked the woman for taking care of my children. While I was there I thanked her without ceasing.

It pained my heart to leave them there for the night, but I had to because it was very late. I said to my husband in front of her, "I would like to have my kids tomorrow," and I told her "Please pack all their clothes because I am taking the kids back to my mother." I said to her "Do you love my husband?" She said yes. I said "O.k. I will divorce him, so you can have him." My husband was so puzzled. So I said "Thanks again. Please bring my children early the next day so that I can travel down to my mother with them."

Not a word from any of them. No fights, no exchange of words between me and them, they both agreed I could have the kids the next day. When I saw she was pregnant, all that kept going in my head was one word - divorce.

After I said what I had to say, I made sure Christ was seen in me to the end. I didn't know if God was pleased when I asked for a divorce, but I did it. I said to God that same night "Lord I am sorry I have to go that route, it would be best." My husband offered to take me back to my sister's, so we got a taxi, and I said "Goodbye see you tomorrow," to the kids. Oh they were so happy. I did say bye to the lady and off we went to my sister's. My husband just dropped me off and he went back with the same taxi.

The next morning bright and early my husband brought the children and they were excited to go back to my mom's with me. So I took my kids back and I noticed my husband had a bag packed for himself. He said "I will go with you and the kids and I will spend a few days and then come back." I said "O.k. no problem." I knew in my heart he would have done that anyhow.

So we all went home to my mother's. My kids had a lot to say to me; they weren't fed well, they had to fetch water from the creek, but I told them they had to forgive the woman and their father, since that is what God asks us to do.

My husband kept hearing from me while he was there that I wanted a divorce. He wasn't happy about this, but that is all I wanted in that moment. I thought "With her being pregnant, he will have two sets of children. No, this can't be, I must divorce." I said to him "I have to return to Canada in a couple of months and I need the divorce before I leave." I also told him he could not take back my kids to his lady anymore; they will stay with my mother until I send for them. He gave me his word that he would not take them from my mother again, and he was sorry that he did.

In the mean time I was trying very hard to let Christ be seen in me. So I said to my husband "I would like to start the divorce in a couple of days because it might take a while and I am going back to Canada." He started to say ok and asked if he came to Canada in the future whether I would remarry him. I said yes, but really I didn't mean it, but I wanted a divorce, that is why I said it. If I didn't say yes he wouldn't give me a divorce. I really repented, because I knew what was in my heart. I wanted out of the marriage and that's it. The divorce started and I did all I had to do. I paid for it and everything. He did what he had to do also, and within a couple of months, I was divorced. I kept repenting all the time because I know God hates divorce.

Matthew 5:31-32 It hath been said, Whosoever shall put away his wife, let him give her a writing of divorcement: But I say unto you, That whosoever shall put away his wife, saving for the cause of fornication, causeth her to commit adultery: and whosoever shall marry her that is divorced committeth adultery.

While I was there he and the woman split up and I knew it was all a big show and that he would continue once I boarded the plane. All in all he had three children with 2 different women. But God gave me the grace. I begged him never to take my children away from my mother again. He did promise me. I said to him "If you don't want to support them, it is ok. I will take care of my children. He did promise he would do his best.

The time came when I had to leave Guyana to return to Canada. My heart bled to part with my kids again. But I prayed and prayed and God gave me the strength once again. I left them with my mother, and that was very comforting. I had gotten all my cousins' addresses from their families in Guyana before I left for Canada.

BACK IN CANADA

When I arrived in Canada it was different from the first time. I now knew more about the place. Once in Toronto, I lived with my cousin and his wife for a while. They were very kind to me. I got a job as a housekeeper, and I would go visit my cousins on the weekend. I have a lot of cousins here in Toronto. I visited with all of them when I could. I continued in the word and prayer. I went to church and I got to know more and more people. God is always so very faithful. He is an awesome God. I worked and I went to school, I did a few courses, all nursing related, and I served God with my whole heart.

Psalm 100:2 Serve the Lord with gladness: come before his presence with singing

I left that job as a housekeeper and I worked at a nursing home, where I was in charge of 76 mentally ill patients. I love people, irrespective of color, I love rich and poor. I love to work with the sick. God had blessed me with his Agape love. God is love. I thank God for his love.

John 13:35 By this shall all men know that ye are my disciples, if ye have love one to another.

A Chance
Encounter

In 1975 I met a man at the Eaton's Centre, in downtown Toronto. It was like love at first sight. I always said I would never remarry. This man had a disability, and he invited me to coffee. He asked me if I was married, and I said "Yes I was married and I also have three children, and am divorced." Right there he asked "Will you marry me?" I replied "I am a Christian and I have to pray about that." He asked me for my phone number, and I gave him mine. He told me he had a car accident and he got badly hurt, and that is the reason he walked like that. It wasn't anything big, but you could notice it if you looked at him carefully. I would tell him about the Lord and I would tell him how God can heal him. But he didn't have any interest in the things of God. I don't know if he was bitter from the accident he had or what. I really liked him. He was Canadian, a white man, very handsome, and caring. He loved me a lot, and I did love him too.

As we continued to see each other, he kept asking me to marry him. He also was married before, and divorced, but he didn't have any children. I said to him "If you want children, I can't have any kids for you because I do not want my kids to grow up with step brothers and sisters." He agreed that he would not bother me about having children. He said all he wanted was to marry me. I felt so sorry for this man. Every time I saw him he would cry and cry and he kept saying "I really would like to marry you. Please don't say no." We got along very well. He is soft spoken. I prayed about it, and I got no affirmation. All I think about are his tears. No one in the church knew my story because I never said much.

Ecclesiastes 3:1 There is a time for everything, and a season for every activity under heaven:

A year after I met him, I decided this can't go on like this. So we got married in 1976 and everything went well. I had a very good marriage, but his condition was getting worse. Although you could hardly notice the disability before, now it was very noticeable. But I purposed in my heart no matter what happened, I would continue to be for him what I should be to him, and that is a wife.

Colossians 3:12 Put on therefore, as the elect of God, holy and beloved, bowels of mercies, kindness, humbleness of mind, meekness, longsuffering;

My mother brought my children to Canada in September 1978. Gary was 11, Bruce was 9, and Gail was 8. The kids really liked him. Every thing was just fine. Out of the blues he told me (I think it was 1980) "You have such a nice family and you work so hard." He told me he knew that his situation health wise was getting worse and he said to me it was very unfair of me to take care of him with two or three jobs. I said to him "No, you are not a burden to me." That was the plain truth.

Oh I cried so much; I really did care for him. He said to me "If you truly care, then listen to me. Let us divorce and I will go back to my mother she will take care of me. We can be good friends, and you will not have such a hectic life." She was home all the time. I told him "No you are not a burden." And he went on and on. I am not going to say it was easy. He was very good to me. I was also good to him. I made sure his meals and everything were prepared. Finally I made up my mind to go through with the divorce. But my heart was breaking. It was not easy. I prayed earnestly for the grace and the strength, and I gave him the divorce, and he went back to his mom in around October 1980.

When he left, the children & I were still in the church, and the children were in Sunday school. I made sure I brought up my kids in the ways of the Lord.

Proverbs 22:6 Train up a child in the way he should go: and when he is old, he will not depart from it.

Early in 1981, my ex-husband Dennis phoned me (the father of my children). I asked him how he was doing, and he said "Fine." Then I said hold on, I will let the kids speak to you," because he would normally phone to speak with the kids. After he had finished speaking to the kids he said he would like to speak to me. I said "Ok, fine." Taking the phone from my kids I asked my ex "What you would like to talk to me about?" He said he would like to come to Canada to visit the kids. In my mind I said "This is real soap opera here." I said to him, "Give me one month to fast and pray."

I was growing in the Lord and I didn't know too much, but I was really trying. My mother brought up my kids to Canada, so she was going back to Guyana. I missed her so much. I had a very busy life. I worked at 2 and 3 jobs a day. I lived in a three bedroom apartment in York Mills. I had to carry the rent, and look after my 3 children. I had car payments, insurance, and I had to put food on the table. I made sure I looked after my mother, so I sent money for her every month. My mother was a peach, and she was very good to my kids. So I made sure I sent it, even though my kids were with me. I continued to send money for my mother each month.

Proverbs 22:9 He that hath a bountiful eye shall be blessed; for he giveth of his bread to the poor.

I taught my children to study the word everyday. I taught them the ways of the Lord, I taught them to pray everyday. I was very strict with my kids. I screened what they watched on television. They were not allowed to watch all types of cartoons; especially the ones with magic and the ones with witches etc. I did private nursing from the time I quit that job at the nursing home with mentally ill patients. Long before my kids came, I had stopped working at the nursing home, and then I worked in private nursing. I had three patients so I was from one job to the next. I would get up early in the morning to pray, and then I would cook for my kids before I went to work. Throughout the day they would have food and lots of snacks. I taught them how to bathe themselves. They had a lot to learn and real fast, but they did it. They had to study the word before they did their homework. I always taught my children to put God first, in accordance with what Jesus commanded.

Matthew 6:33 But seek ye first the kingdom of God, and his righteousness; and all these things shall be added unto you.

I would mark their Bible Study when I came home at night. I always gave them a good or a very good mark to encourage them. I would anoint my children mornings before they went to school, and I would anoint them every night before they slept. They were very good children. And the glory goes to God.

At this point I had to phone my ex husband about coming up to see my children. I phoned my ex husband and I told him he could come, because I knew he didn't have a place to stay. He has a lot of family here, but like me when I first came, I had lots of family but I didn't know where they were living. On my second trip I knew a lot more. It was the same with him, he had lots of family but he didn't know where they lived. But I remembered what I went through, and how God made a way for me.

2 Samuel 22:33 God is my strength and power: and he maketh my way perfect.

The first job I called, I got it. That woman took me in, I had my own room and everything. God made that way for me. So I thought "Well let me tell him to come." I said to him "O.K. you can come, but I have some conditions. I am a Christian," and I reminded him of when I went home to pay my kids a visit. I told him from that nothing has changed, I am still a Christian, and I cannot have anything to do with him, because we are divorced. I said to him on the phone "I do not intend to remarry you. I do not play. I am very serious with my walk with God. I will not live a double standard life. I fear God, and I hate sin with a passion. I will prepare a room for you, I will cook for you. I will wash your clothes, I will do everything but can't go further than that. You have to respect me. I am not prepared to do it another way. Now, if you can abide by these rules, you are welcome. If you can't abide by these rules, please do not come. I am just trying to help you and when you get on your two feet, you will have to move out. I am very sorry, but this is the way it has to be. Now, if you need time to think, that is fine. If you would like to give me an answer right now that is fine also." He said immediately "I will abide by all your rules." I said "O.K. you are free to come."

At this point my children and I were serving God more than ever. I made sure the children studied the word of God every day. I taught them how to pray and how to do spiritual warfare in their own little way; I taught them at their own level. I tried to tell them as Christians their light must shine.

Matthew 5:16 Let your light so shine before men, that they may see your good works, and glorify your Father which is in heaven.

They cannot get into fights at school; they have to respect their teachers. The way they carry themselves at school must be very Christ-like; they must not touch drugs or alcohol or cigarettes, they must not tell lies and they must not get into any types of mischief or swearing. Kids that indulged in these things could not be their friends.

1 Peter 2:11 Beloved, I beg *you* as sojourners and pilgrims, abstain from fleshly lusts which war against the soul

THE OLD CHURCH

With regards to the church where we attended, I am sorry, but I can't mention names or addresses of churches, or names of preachers. I cannot. Please bear with me but there are things that I will have to say, that are not pleasant. I faced a lot in this church. I truly believed the preacher did like me. Or maybe I can say one of the women he was after. He was married, he had children, and they were a nice family. I couldn't understand why he would want to live that life. More so he was a preacher. I knew he slept with women that were going to the church. I can honestly say that verbally he never one day said to me "I like you." He never said anything out of line. Never. Never. You may wonder how I knew this man liked me. I knew. The Spirit of God would reveal a lot of things to me. I know for a fact without the Holy Spirit I am dead. There are three things with my walk with God that I really love.

1. Praying is my hobby. I know this sounds way out. But the Lord bears witness to this. I like to pray early in the mornings from about 3 a.m. to 5 a.m. sometimes more than that. This time is usually in intercession as the Spirit leads.

2. I also love the Word of God. I love to study the Bible. Over and over again from Genesis to Revelation, I have studied it. I like two versions; the Old King James Version and the Amplified version, but I don't really use the Amplified version very much. Very rarely. I love the King James. The Word of God says

Psalms 119:11 Thy word have I hid in mine heart, that I might not sin against thee.

The word of God also says we must pray without ceasing

1 Thessalonians 5:17 Pray without ceasing.

I love fasting also; fasting does a lot. Jesus taught about fasting when his disciples could not cast out the demons. Jesus told them about their unbelief, and he told them about their faithlessness. Then Jesus said to them:

Matthew 17:21 Howbeit this kind goeth not out but by prayer and fasting.

I love all three, but praying is my hobby. When I was working for the secular world I had two and three jobs. I would take my vacation and not go anywhere. When I took my vacation leave, it was just to seek the Lord, and spend quality time in His presence, fasting and praying.

By the grace of God, I am an intercessor.

I thank God for fasting. It kills the flesh. If I wasn't fasting the devil would have his way. But Glory be to God, every time I see a danger zone, I run for my life. God is able to keep.

1 Thessalonians 5:22 Abstain from all appearance of evil.

The preacher was an excellent teacher; he knew the Word of God, and would expound well on the word. I believe every sermon he preached was about me. I would love to share some of his sermons to let you know where I was coming from, but I can't.

I will let you in on one of them. It came at a time he had to leave; another preacher was going to take over. So before that preacher went, he preached this message: "Let no man steal your crown." I knew exactly where he was coming from. He couldn't mess with my crown and no one else must mess with it. My God my God, help us. He left and someone else took over. I was still there with my children.

My ex-husband came up to Canada in 1981. After he came, we continued there in that church for a while, and the Lord led me into a forty days fast. I only had liquids in this fast; nothing to eat, but I drank a lot of liquids. The Lord spoke loud and clear. He said "Jean, you have to move with your children from this church to another one" and the Lord clearly gave me the name of the other church I had to go to with my kids. The church was in the west and I lived in the east, but I have learned to obey God for the scriptures say that obedience is better than sacrifice.

1 Samuel 15:22 And Samuel said, Hath the LORD as great delight in burnt offerings and sacrifices, as in obeying the voice of the LORD? Behold, to obey is better than sacrifice, and to hearken than the fat of rams.

The New Church

M e and my children started to go to the new church. We attended this church for about 8 years. This church was very interesting and so much was going on. I loved the church. The Lord said "I want you to be an intercessor in this church." I never said much. But I would watch and pray.

Mark 13:33 Take ye heed, watch and pray: for ye know not when the time is.

I didn't allow my children in the young people's group. I didn't allow my children to partake in a lot of things, because the leaders of these groups were not living and walking pure. I did not want my children to be contaminated; I didn't want spirits to be transferred to them. Being an intercessor in that church, a lot was revealed to me by the Spirit. I was in the bus ministry and I was on the soul winning team. I was very involved, but only behind the scenes. The pulpit was not right, leaders like elders were not living pure, there was a lot of adultery and fornication, and even in the choir many were not living right. I was very grieved, but I stayed true to what God called me there for.

I would invite my ex-husband to church but he would not budge. By this time he had found a job and had settled in. I must say he behaved himself well. Sometimes we would exchange words. However, like the scripture says I try to let my words be few.

Ecclesiastes 5:2 Be not rash with thy mouth, and let not thine heart be hasty to utter any thing before God: for God is in heaven, and thou upon earth: therefore let thy words be few.

Many times the arguments were for silly little things. He loves his daughter a lot, and he spoilt her rotten. At this point I still had three children, two boys, and one girl. He would ask his daughter to watch cartoons that I did not approve of. All these things I told him about when he came in. The cartoons with witches and all kinds of magic and such - I didn't let my kids look at them - he would call his daughter to watch the very things I didn't like. I brought up my children very strict. So I started a forty days fast. And I said "God, he has to go. Please Lord,

give me a time so when I tell him to leave I would also give him a time."
I will never forget, for as long as I live, what I am about to say.

The Lord's Request

One morning in that fast, about a little more than half way in the fast, the Spirit of God said to me "Jean go out on the balcony." I was living in a 3 bedroom apartment and I gave my ex-husband my daughter's room, when he came in the country. I took in my daughter to share my bedroom. That morning I got up to go to the washroom about 2:55am. The Lord said "Go out on the balcony." I made sure I covered my daughter well because she kicks off the covers all the time. I said "God, o.k., I will go on the balcony." As soon as I was out on the balcony I started to worship and praise the Lord. Then I started to feel a bit uncomfortable, but I knew the reason. I had on a purple night gown, and the neck was a low cut, with spaghetti straps.

Psalm 135:1 Praise ye the LORD. Praise ye the name of the LORD; praise him, O ye servants of the LORD.

I don't like to go in the presence of the Lord like that. Many will find this to be weird, but that is the way I am. So I rushed inside, and I put on a little light sweater because it was summer. I started to praise and worship God on that balcony like nobody's business, and I could feel the presence of God very strong. Out of the blues the Lord spoke to me. He said Jean "I want you to remarry Dennis." (My ex-husband's name is Dennis.) I said "God are you for real? God I don't even love this man. How can I remarry him? You are asking me to do something that does not line up with your word. This man is not saved. We would be unequally yoked."

I stormed in the apartment, and I got my Bible. I sat on the chair at the dining table, put on the lights and I opened my Bible and it opened to Hosea. I didn't have to search for anything because I was about to remind God of what His word says.

2 Corinthians 6:14 Be ye not unequally yoked together with unbelievers: for what fellowship hath righteousness with unrighteousness? and what communion hath light with darkness?

But when I opened the Bible it flew open to Hosea. I started to read Hosea. I got to the second verse of chapter one, God said to Hosea:

Hosea 1:2-3 The beginning of the word of the LORD by Hosea. And the LORD said to Hosea, Go, take unto thee a wife of whoredoms and children of whoredoms: for the land hath committed great whoredom, departing from the LORD. So he went and took Gomer the daughter of Diblaim; which conceived, and bare him a son.

So I started to really cry, and I repented. And I said "God, Hosea is a prophet. I am just an ordinary woman sitting in the pew. I am so sorry Lord. The prophet obeyed you and married the prostitute. Who am I? I will obey you and remarry him. But just remember Lord, I don't love him. You will have to give me that love for him."

There are some very tough things that God would ask of me. Trust me, this is one of them. I have learned from the scriptures that obedience is better than sacrifice. I would rather die than disobey God knowingly. I called up a preacher from the directory, and we went to his house. On my way to the preacher's house, I stopped in to see my sister. (Then she lived in Canada, now she lives in London, England). I stopped there, and I borrowed a plain gold ring from her. (I had spoken to her before about borrowing it, so she knew what I was going to do with the ring). I had on my white uniform, because right after I was married, I had to go to work. So with a borrowed ring and with my white uniform on, we went to the preacher's house. The ceremony lasted five minutes. I was so upset because I had to remarry him, and I did not want to. I didn't even buy a ring; I could have bought a nice little ring. But I said "No, I will borrow my sister's." He couldn't care less. All he wanted was to get married. After we got married, I drove my husband home, dropped him off in the lobby, and I drove off and went to work.

We got married seven months after he came to Canada - something I never wanted. I did it because I love God. When I got to work, I cried so much, and I felt so convicted, and I knew it was because of the way I did things. The conviction was killing me.

When I came home from work I had my shower. I gave everybody their dinner, because I cooked before I went to get married, so I just had to heat it up and serve. I said to my kids and my husband "I do not want to be disturbed." I went in my room and I knelt down and I repented to God, I cried out to God and I really repented. I was in His presence for about three hours. Then I came out of my room. I told my husband how sorry I was for the way I did things. I hugged my three children and I prayed with them. I even said sorry to all my kids (I don't know why, but I said sorry to them). I made sure I left no stone unturned. God is so good, he gave me a peace about the marriage, it was awesome.

God sure had a sense of humor, later on down the road. The Lord told me to renew my vows, but this time I bought a ring and it was blessed by the minister, who renewed our vows. This man of God was Pentecostal and had nothing to do with my Pastor. For many reasons I thank God for the way he did it. When God calls the shots you can't go wrong. For one year straight I didn't say much to my husband. I only spoke if I had to. With my children I acted as if everything was normal. I would sit and ponder things.

Now that we were married I kept asking my husband to go to church with me. He would make all kinds of promises Saturday. On Sunday the story changed to "I don't feel like it." I would not say a word. I didn't fight; I don't nag him in anyway, but I kept praying for his soul.

I used to work for a doctor in psychology; he was one of my patients. When my husband came to Canada and settled in, when he started to work I gave up all other jobs, but I kept this one. The doctor and his wife were very nice to me.

I worked there for seven years and the doctor had a partial stroke. I witnessed to this man about Jesus all the time. They were from Germany. His wife was a staunch Anglican. I would read the scriptures to him, I would pray for him, and I would sing for him. Oh he loved the songs. He loved Amazing Grace. As I continued to witness to him, telling him about the goodness of God, and how much Jesus loves him, one day he really began weeping and he said to me "I am ready to accept Jesus as my Lord and Saviour." The stroke affected his speech very little. You could understand every word he spoke. The glory of God filled the home that day. It was so glorious. In the seventh year I was working there, he accepted the Lord, and a little after that he died. This was extremely difficult for me, after all, seven years is not seven months. But I comforted myself with one thing; he made Heaven his home.

John 11:26 And whosover liveth and believeth in me shall never die. Believest thou this?

THE NEXT REQUESTS

The Lord said to me: "Jean I want you to stop working. I don't want you to get a part time job, or a full time job." I went on a forty days fast. I started to seek God as to why I should stop working. I have lived a fasted life all my life, even up to this day as I am writing this book. Fasting is a lifestyle for me. I love it. You would never know when I am fasting. I never lose weight; I am one way all the time. To God Be the Glory.

Isaiah 58:6 Is not this the fast that I have chosen? to loose the bands of wickedness, to undo the heavy burdens, and to let the oppressed go free, and that ye break every yoke?

Prior to the doctor's death for many years I would have dreams and visions about preaching to large crowds. Many times in those dreams and visions people would be healed. I would see the dead raised, the lame walk and the blind see. I used to write them all down in a little book.

In that same 40 day fast I was on after the doctor died, on day number 35, God spoke to me audibly for the first time. On this fast I was a bit weak, because all I had was liquids; I couldn't have anything to eat. On day 35 I took some pillows and put them behind me. I sat up in bed with a pillow on my lap, and I was reading the book of Revelation. Normally before I go into prayer I like to read and study the word first. At about 7pm on day number 35 of the fast this voice spoke to me and said "Jean, I want you to build a church on your mother's land, but your sister will preach in that church. You will also build a missionary home with 4 bedrooms in it. And it must be a two storey building. Upstairs must have all four bedrooms and downstairs must have the kitchen and living room." And He clearly told me that my sister must live in that house after it is built. This sister was saved long before me - many years before. And when she used to witness to me I would tell it like it is. But God is so merciful to me. I did not understand any of this myself. I knew it was God and it was amazing.

I went to the pastor of the church I was attending, and I said "God spoke to me about building a church and I would really like some answers." I told him I was on this fast and day number 35 of the fast the Lord spoke loud and clear and He said to me "Jean I want you to build a church on your Mother's land." Of course I didn't know much, so I said "Pastor how can this be, when I am not even a preacher?" I barely finished the statement when he said "God would never call a woman to build a church. He would call your husband to build a church." So I said to him "Pastor, how would God call my husband to build a church and he is not saved?" He said "Well, I know God would not call a woman to build a church." I didn't even get to tell him about the missionary home, or about my sister. I said very nicely to him "Thank you Pastor for your time. Bye."

As from that day, I never felt the same about him. I had a lot of questions, and I pondered them for years. I never said anything to anyone. My children and I kept attending the church. I wanted to leave right then, but the Lord said "No. I am not finished with you here." I cried and cried, but I asked God to give me the grace and the strength to continue. Oh I loved this man of God so much with the love of Jesus and I still do.

Visions and Dreams

Acts 2:17 And it shall come to pass in the last days, saith God, I will pour out of my Spirit upon all flesh: and your sons and your daughters shall prophesy, and your young men shall see visions, and your old men shall dream dreams:

Then a couple years after this I had a dream with him. I did not want to go to him, but the Lord said "Go to him and tell him the dream."

Just before I had the dream with the Pastor, I dreamt my school mate died. In real life this girl and I were very close friends at school and she would always come to get me and we would go to Sunday school together; she loves the Lord. I dreamt that she came to me in a dream and she said to me: "Jean, God has called you to a healing ministry; it is going to be world wide. Do your very best, it is going to be very big." And then I woke up.

In reality I tried to find out if my friend died, and people would tell me "Yes she died." About one week after I dreamt this, I dreamt about the Pastor. This is what I dreamt. I was in Guyana in my mother's old house where I was born and where I grew up. Our kitchen door is in 2 halves. We always kept the bottom half closed. We always opened the top half. I was at the kitchen door standing and I saw a funeral passing, it didn't reach in front of our house yet, but it was slowly approaching the house. We had a little veranda by the front door. So to get to this veranda, I had to walk through the little living room, to go open the front door and then go out the door and stand on the veranda (where I would see everything better).

So in the dream I went and stood on the veranda, and at this time the casket was right opposite our house and at the funeral procession was a very large crowd. In the dream as I stood on the veranda, I stretched my hands out to this casket that was passing on the road, and I said these words three times. "Lord if you have given me a healing ministry, like my friend told me in that dream, then raise that dead up that is passing now." I saw with my eyes in the dream the lid of the casket went up just a little bit, and it went down back again. Then I said the second time, Lord if you called me to a healing ministry like my friend told me in that dream then raise this dead that is passing. The lid went a little higher than the first time, and it went back down again. Now in the dream I did not know who had died; I did not know who was in that casket.

The third time I stretched my hands out towards the casket, and I said "Lord, if you did call me to a healing ministry like my friend said to me in the dream I had with her about a week ago, raise this dead up that is passing in Jesus name." And the lid of the casket fully opened this time, and the Pastor walked out of the casket. While he was coming out of the casket I went to the kitchen, took the broom, and I started to sweep the kitchen when I got to the door I opened it to sweep out the dust and I saw the pastor walking up the stairs to come into the kitchen. So I stopped sweeping, and I said "Pastor, please come in. So you were dead, and God raised you up." And then my eyes opened from the dream.

I did go to the pastor to share this dream, and I asked him what it meant. I knew what the dream meant, but because God said "Go share the dream with him" I went. I can remember very well, he had a very sad look on his face, and he never answered me, not one word. Then I said "Pastor, maybe another time. Bye pastor."

I know for sure he listened to every word of that dream very keenly but he was very sad. I never went back to him about anything until the end when they kicked me and my family out of the church; I will explain that later.

GIVE GOD YOUR BEST

I wish I had a pastor that I could sit and talk to. I wish I had a pastor so that if I had a question, or a dream or vision, or an encounter with God, I could go and talk to him. Or if I had a need for him to talk to my children for any reason or make an appointment with him so he could talk to my unsaved husband. I never had any of this. I paid my tithes faithfully. Every time my husband got paid he would sign his cheque and give it to me (even though my husband was not going to church). I took 1/10 out of that money (I paid tithes for my husband), and I never told him I did that until when we left. I gave my all. I didn't pay 10%. I gave ½ my paycheck, and 10% of my husband's tithes. But thank God I paid tithes as unto the Lord, not to man. I did it with my whole heart. I know if I did not pay tithes I would be cursed and my family would be cursed because the bible says so. You are either blessed or cursed.

Malachi 3:8-12 Will a man rob God? Yet ye have robbed me. But ye say, Wherein have we robbed thee? In tithes and offerings. Ye are cursed with a curse: for ye have robbed me, even this whole nation. Bring ye all the tithes into the storehouse, that there may be meat in mine house, and prove me now herewith, saith the LORD of hosts, if I will not open you the windows of heaven, and pour you out a blessing, that there shall not be room enough to receive it. And I will rebuke the devourer for your sakes, and he shall not destroy the fruits of your ground; neither shall your vine cast her fruit before the time in the field, saith the LORD of hosts. And all nations shall call you blessed: for ye shall be a delightsome land, saith the LORD of hosts.

The reason why I brought up tithes is because I would like everyone who reads this book to know that no matter what you are going through in a church, once God has placed you there, keep your eyes on Jesus. I believe all God's children should seek God for His perfect will where they go to church. You don't go to church just for convenience. Just because a church is ½ a block from your house is that where you go? No - you ask God for divine direction and you follow those directions to the letter.

Proverbs 3:5-6 Trust in the LORD with all thine heart; and lean not unto thine own understanding. In all thy ways acknowledge him, and he shall direct thy paths.

You don't jump all over the globe, and when you do find God's perfect will, wherever God places you be very faithful to the end. You may have a pastor who is a great man or a great woman of God; praise God for that. On the other hand, you can have a pastor who preaches the word but doesn't quite live up to the word, and stay true. Many times you might be tempted to run, but wait until you get the green light from God. Just like me, God wanted to make me into that precious pearl that he wanted me to be. Remember he is the potter and we are the clay. If you are persecuted, take it gracefully. If you feel rejected or hated or despised don't go all over the church or all over the globe and talk about it, and don't stop paying tithes either, because you don't want to live under curses.

Not paying tithes is a sin. I have never read in God's word that a thief will enter into Heaven. With any sin in your life, God says in His word that because of your sin He will not hear when you pray (until you genuinely repent).

Isaiah 59:1-3 Behold, the LORD's hand is not shortened, that it cannot save; neither his ear heavy, that it cannot hear: But your iniquities have separated between you and your God, and your sins have hid his face from you, that he will not hear. For your hands are defiled with blood, and your fingers with iniquity; your lips have spoken lies, your tongue hath muttered perverseness.

The problems in the church will either make you or break you. Not only are people tempted to not pay tithes when they are going through problems in a church - people tend to want to run. I have some serious advice for you. Once God places you there and you want to run, pray and ask God if he wants that. If you do walk out of God's perfect will, I guarantee you that you will backslide. This is very serious. If you are a family person, all your family could backslide. God would not be able to trust you with anything because you can't handle heat. I say all these things to say this; stay true, stay faithful, and keep your focus and your eyes fixed on Jesus. If not, you will run.

So many times I wanted to run but God would not give me the green light. So many times I could have stopped paying tithes and I could have become so bitter, but glory to God He blessed me with the grace. I fear God so much. When it comes to being in the centre of God's will I endured and endured, and when I was kicked out, I knew beyond a shadow of a doubt that was the time I had to leave. Now I am not saying stay in your church until you are kicked out. I am not saying that at all. That is the way it went with me. But all of us are different. Once God places you there, He has a plan for you there. Don't let anything or anyone run you out. Let God do it. And He does it beautifully. Praise God.

It is such a glorious honor to bear the marks of the Lord Jesus in my body. I count it the highest honor and I count it the highest privilege to suffer for Jesus' sake. I will Glory in the Cross, so that the power of God will rest on me.

I continued to ponder all these dreams. I had lots and lots of dreams. I could not go back to my pastor, so I wrote all my visions and all my dreams down.

Trust and Obey

One day the phone rang and it was the doctor's wife. Though he passed away, his wife used to call me now and again on the phone. She said to me "Jean, I have a friend who is very sick, and I told my friend's daughter that you would be the ideal person to work for her mom, because you are so kind, loving, and very patient. This woman wants you to come for an interview. I would like you to take the phone number and call them to set up an appointment. Please Jean, try to help them out." I told her "Thanks for everything." I called the number she gave me. I introduced myself on the phone and she set up the appointment to see me, and I went. I met with the sick lady's daughter. She seemed to be a very nice person. When she was finished with me, she took me to be introduced to her mother, and I got the job. That patient died after 7 weeks.

My husband said "Sorry but you will have to find another job." The daughter of the woman that died gave my phone number to one of her friends, and that friend called me, and asked if I could come for an interview. My husband overheard the conversation and he said "You have to go. You can't afford not to work." Oh, he persecuted me day and night. I went to the job interview and this time the lady's husband had cancer. I got the job and I started to work. This patient died after seven weeks. I said "God you really want me to stop working. It is very clear."

After this patient died they gave my number out to a member of their family that was sick. The man called me for an interview and I went and I got the job, this man's wife had cancer, and she died after 7 weeks. After this patient died I said "Ok, God I heard you loud and clear, this is it. Enough is enough. Just give me the grace and the strength to stand up to my husband." I said to my husband "I need to talk to you for a few minutes. The doctor died after I worked there 7 years. God said I am not to go back to work. I took 3 other patients because you kept pressuring me to go back to work, and all three patients died after seven weeks each." My husband said "You still have to go to work" and he kept persecuting me. I said to him "I am not prepared to listen to you anymore. If you don't like it you may leave. But now I will listen to God not you. I cannot do this anymore - even the blind can see that God does not want me to work, look at how things are going with all these deaths, one after the other. That's it."

Acts 5:29 Then Peter and the other apostles answered and said, We ought to obey God rather than men.

I went on a forty day fast and I repented and I said "Lord I am so sorry to disobey you." I really cried out to God. And my husband kept persecuting me. One night he said he would leave. "I can help you to pack" I said. I packed his clothes and I took the 2 suitcases to him. I said "Goodbye! I would rather you go, but I will not disobey God anymore."

Proverbs 24:26 Every man shall kiss his lips that giveth a right answer.

He started towards the door and when he got to the door the Holy Ghost took this man on his knees and God started to deal with him right there. He was crying like a baby. He cried for more than one hour straight and then he came back inside (so he didn't go). I said to him "Let me live in peace and do my Father's will and if you continue to persecute me I will go with my kids." He said he was sorry. After one week he started up again.

An Unexpected Illness

I wasn't feeling well. I was sick every morning for a week. I watched it and I decided to go to the doctor for a check up. They took a pregnancy test. The doctor said he would call me after a couple days. When the call came, he said "Jean you are pregnant." I didn't have an easy pregnancy, it was always very rough. Now I know for sure that God had to allow this because with the baby I couldn't go to work; I was 35 years old. I went to the doctor and they said I should have an abortion because of my age and this and that will happen with the baby. I turned and I said to the nurse "You would not understand this language but I have been walking in rebellion against God for the past few months and of course the very thing I never wanted has happened to me now." I knew this is pay day. "Now you are telling me I should have an abortion? Not only was I walking in rebellion but now you want me to commit murder. I will have my baby even if it means my death." She asked "You really mean this?" I said yes. She said "I don't understand what you are saying about this rebellion thing against God." I said "You will not understand because the natural man does not understand the things of God, for it is foolishness to them."

1 Corinthians 2:14 But the natural man receiveth not the things of the Spirit of God: for they are foolishness unto him: neither can he know them, because they are spiritually discerned.

I said to her "This is plain English, I will not abort my baby, if it means my death." She said "Ok. But..." "But nothing. Goodbye, see you on my next appointment." My husband was very happy when I got pregnant. We already had two boys and one girl. Now this was the fourth one, and he said he wanted a girl. My third child was 14 years old when I got pregnant with this one. For the whole 9 months I was very sick. Everything I ate came back up. I purposed in my heart no matter how sick I was I would study the word of God from Genesis to Revelation. I would pray and study the word. During this pregnancy

I had a lot of dreams of preaching, and the sick being healed and so forth. I would write them down.

MARBLES

One day I was very sick. I decided I would try and shower and go right back on the sofa to lie down, and off I went to sleep. I had a profound dream. I was about five months pregnant when I had this dream. At about 2 pm that day I dreamt I was back home in Guyana at my mother's house. I went out on the road and I saw Jesus. He appeared to me very ordinarily. He had on a robe; it had one pocket at the right side of the robe at the top (like how a shirt has pockets).

So I began to walk with Him, and we were talking. I cannot remember anything we talked about. In real life my mother's house is not far in from the road. In this dream as we were walking, my sister was cleaning up the yard. I could hear her very plainly from the road. She was calling my mother and said "Ma come and see who Jean is walking with. Come quickly she is walking with Jesus." I heard that but I never said anything. As I continued to walk with Him we came up to a little child playing marbles. This child had 6 marbles. The most beautiful marbles I have ever seen. The marbles were very colourful, and were sparkling. So this child had one marble on the ground and he had 5 in his little hands. Jesus took the 5 marbles from the child (Jesus had asked him first.) The child gave Him the 5 marbles. Jesus took 4 marbles and put them in his pocket, like I said, there was a pocket on the right side of His robe at the top. And the fifth marble Jesus had in his hand was used to pitch the marble to hit the other one that was already on the ground. As He was pitching this marble he was in a bent position and all 4 of the marbles fell out of his pocket. When the marbles fell out of his pocket I picked up all four and put them back in his pocket. Then I woke up from the dream. I said Lord "I wish someone would call me that could interpret this dream for me."

1 John 5:14-15 And this is the confidence that we have in him, that if we ask any thing according to his will, he heareth us: And if we know that he hear us, whatsoever we ask, we know that we have the petitions that we desired of him

While I was saying that to the Lord the phone rang. I had this friend in church; we worked on the bus ministry together. I said "I just had a dream." She said "Tell me about it" so I told her the dream. She said "Jean this is so easy. The four marbles that fell out of Jesus' pocket represents the four corners of the world. The roundness of the marble you can liken to the world, and you picking up the marbles and putting them back in His pocket means God will send you to the four corners of this world to preach the gospel and you will bring many souls to the Lord." It was so unique the way she interpreted the dream; it was quite something - the presence of God came down in a powerful way upon me. I had to go and sit down on the sofa quickly, or else I would have been slain in the spirit. What an awesome God. This made me begin to think why God wanted me to stop working. So many times in the pregnancy the nurses and doctors had so much to say - a lot of the stuff was way out. But God brought me through that pregnancy.

My Healer

At the hospital, I had the baby in three hours. This was the only child that I delivered so quickly. The other three children came within 8 to 15 hours. Jesus makes all the difference. When I had the first three children I wasn't a Christian, but when I had this one, I was a Christian for 11 years already. My baby was very normal, and I give God all the Glory and the Praise. She was about 7lbs and she was born in September 1984. Her name is Tricia, and she is a great blessing. My husband was so happy; he wanted a girl and God came in. So we have 2 boys and 2 girls. She is now 24 years old and from the time she was born until the day of the writing of this book 24 years have gone by and I have never gone to a doctor not even to check my blood pressure or even to have a checkup. God is my healer, God keeps me. I do get sick (the common cold) or sometimes I do feel a little weak from the fasting, but God takes care of everything. One Sunday evening I came home from church, I had my shower and I had something hot to drink. I felt a chest pain and the devil said "Well you have to go to the hospital." I said to the devil "In the name of Jesus get out from my chest and go back to the pits of hell where you came from. I do not serve you and you don't have any right to touch my body with sickness. Get out satan, the blood of Jesus is against you. In Jesus name I am healed."

I took my bible and I opened it to Isaiah 53 and I placed the bible on my chest and quoted from verse 5.

Isaiah 53:5 But he was wounded for our transgressions, he was bruised for our iniquities: the chastisement of our peace was upon him; and with his stripes we are healed.

All the pain went and I've never had a chest pain since then. I don't have a problem with doctors. I don't have a problem if I am sick and have to call the ambulance. If I have to, trust me, I will. I don't have a problem if I have to take two tablets if I have a pain; but I go to God first, I pray and exercise faith in Him, and all the times God comes in for me. Praise God. I got my baby dedicated at the church by the minister and everything went well. Then after that a few months later my husband got saved. This indeed was a great miracle. Salvation is the greatest miracle. There is nothing like it.

LEARNING TO LISTEN

The Lord said to me one day "Jean, you must take your kids out of school." I didn't say anything to my children. I said "God if this is what you want, speak to the children individually. They are old enough and the kids are living a pure life, they pray, they study the word of God, and you can speak to them. When you do, I will take that as a confirmation that I have to take them out."

Judges 6:37-38 Behold, I will put a fleece of wool in the floor; and if the dew be on the fleece only, and it be dry upon all the earth beside, then shall I know that thou wilt save Israel by mine hand, as thou has said.

One day there was a visiting evangelist, and the altar call was for the baptism in the Holy Ghost. One of my kids was filled already and the other one wasn't. He did not go to the altar, but the Spirit of God said "Lay hands on him and pray" (he was sitting right next to me). I just put my hands on his shoulders and he got filled instantly; he was speaking in that heavenly language and was gloriously filled, Praise God. The service was finished and I started to drive. The same one that got filled was really weeping, so I asked him if he was ok and he said "Yes mom." This was on the highway. He said "Mom can you pull the car in that little lane at the very corner and stop for a few minutes? I said "Yes son." I pulled in that lane and put on my four ways, and I stopped. When I stopped he said, "Mom, the Lord is dealing with me about school." I asked "What is the Lord saying?" He said "Mom the Lord does not want me to go back to school." Then the other son said the same thing and the girl said the same thing. So I listened to all three of them in the car.

I said to them "Remember this day. It is not your mother that is taking you out of school. It is God because you guys said that the Lord said so." I told the kids "This is confirmation because God told me to take you all out of school a while ago. And I did ask God to confirm this. Well tonight He did." We gave God thanks and praise in the car, and we prayed. Then I went back to driving to go home. I started to fast and pray, seeking God about what to do with the children and so forth, now they were out of school. The Lord said, "I have called your family as a Levite family. I will set your whole family apart for ministry." I sought God about Bible college for myself and the children. The Lord said "No Bible college." The Holy Ghost will teach us everything as we yield ourselves to Him. We really wanted to go to Bible college and when the Lord said no we were all disappointed; especially the two boys. So we obeyed God.

A Final
Confrontation

One night the Spirit of God moved upon me mightily and the Holy Ghost said "Take a pen with paper and sit and write the pastor a letter, I will give you the words to write" saith the Lord.

I started to write as the Spirit would have me. I wrote seven or eight pages in a note book. From the first line I started to write, I never stopped for a second. I wrote 7 or eight pages non stop. After I was finished with the letter, the Lord said "Put it under the door of his office." I did that; I pushed it under his door. During the same week there was a prayer and bible study on the Thursday morning (it was every Thursday). Another preacher would do that Bible study, so I normally would go every Thursday. That particular Thursday I sat down, and as I was listening to the Word, someone tapped me on my shoulder and called me out of the Bible study and said "Please follow me." He took me to a room with a huge table and chairs around it. I guess that was their boardroom. It had about seven elders around this table. I was fasting and I didn't walk with my handbag, because I didn't know that I would be in a meeting. I had left my handbag where the Bible study was kept. I wanted some tissues and then I realized I didn't have my bag. I sat down throughout the meeting with a vice president in attendance. They spoke to me one after the other - taking turns. The first one asked "Did you write the Pastor a letter?" I replied "Yes, I did because God told me to." They asked me who the Pastor was in adultery with. I told them "I didn't write a letter to any of you. Bring the Pastor and I will give him all the answers to all his questions, if he asked me. But I am sorry I can't deal with you guys. The Pastor is right in the building. Go call him and I will wait for him."

They told me "The Pastor does not want to talk to you." I said "Tell him he can hide from me, but he can't hide from God." Throughout the meeting they were asking some really silly questions. One of them asked "Do you come to the prayer meeting on Saturdays?" I replied "I do every Saturday, I would come in the morning to go and witness and then I stayed back for the prayer meeting in the afternoon, then I go home. Why did you ask?" He answered "I just asked a question." I said to all of them "I have never seen you guys in the prayer meetings. If you were going to the prayer meetings, you would see me there." Because I never missed one prayer meeting they were all very embarrassed. You could see it on their faces. Then they said to me "You nor your husband nor your children are allowed to come back to this church from this day. You did not answer the question we asked." I said "I didn't write a letter to you guys and the Pastor doesn't want to speak to me. I have nothing to say about the man's sins to you." As God is my witness, I am not adding or taking away from what they said; I have a fear for God (beyond words) and I don't like to tell lies. I hate lies.

Proverbs 6:16-19 These six things doth the LORD hate: yea, seven are an abomination unto him: A proud look, a lying tongue, and hands that shed innocent blood, An heart that deviseth wicked imaginations, feet that be swift in running to mischief, A false witness that speaketh lies, and he that soweth discord among brethren. My son, keep thy father's commandment, and forsake not the law of thy mother:

They said to me "If you or your husband or your children are seen on this church property you will be taken bodily off the premises." I said "Ok, I promise you that you will not have any need for that because now that you kicked us out, we won't come back." Don't worry. One of them said "Mrs. Tracey now that you can't come back here, what will you do now?" I said "I will wait on God. Thank you guys for everything. I would like to do two things before I leave. I would like to get my handbag, and I would like to say goodbye to the Pastor and to say thanks to him for the eight years in the church. I just want to give him a hug and say thanks." They told me that they would get my handbag, but I am not allowed to see the Pastor to say anything to him, and I was not allowed near him. I said ok. They gave me my bag and they escorted me to my car. And that was it. And that was December 1987. From that day, up to this day I am writing this book, I have never gone back, not even once. They kicked me out with my family, and I will not go back.

Luke 9:5 And whosoever will not receive you, when ye go out of that city, shake off the very dust from your feet for a testimony against them.

All these events nearly caused my husband to backslide. But God is so good. My children also were very discouraged but God has healed all of them. As for me, I asked God to forgive all the elders and board members and the vice president. God alone knows who were there around that table. I could have seen through them all. I could tell a lot was wrong, but I asked God to forgive the pulpit, I asked God to have mercy on them all. God is God and He will always be God. The word of God says there is nothing hidden that shall not be revealed. God has called me to preach the gospel, and the Lord said I must start to preach to my family in our apartment. I answered the call. I went on a 40 day fast and those were the words I heard. And I said "Yes Lord."

I can honestly say this was extremely difficult for all of us. My husband said "You were so committed, and so faithful in every area of that ministry. You paid your tithes faithfully, you didn't miss a service. You were there for soul winning. Look at the many times you would fast and pray for the minister and many nights labouring in prayer. The bus ministry. Oh how you love the children." He went on and on. I said to him, "Whatever I did, it was not unto man, it was unto God. And God is the one who rewards us." I would sit with my family and talk to them and really encourage them to move on, and I told them they must keep their eyes on Jesus. I would take the word of God, and share the four gospels with them. I told them how much Jesus went through for us, and really, this is nothing to go through for Jesus. I said to them it is the highest honor to suffer for the cause of Christ. What a privilege to bear the marks of the Lord Jesus in my body (see Galatians 6:17).

Matthew 10:38 And he who does not take his cross and follow after Me is not worthy of Me.

2 Timothy 2:12 If we endure, we shall also reign with *Him.* If we deny *Him,* He also will deny us.

I give God all the praise. I prayed for them all. I said to the Lord "If I am wrong, please forgive me, and if they are wrong, please forgive them." I asked the Lord to have mercy on them. Praise God. I love Jesus with all my heart, with all my mind, with all my strength, and with all my soul. If Jesus calls me to go through this again, for me it will be an honor. I did say to the Lord when I got saved, "I want my life to be an open book." The Lord knows our capacity, and He knows how much we can take, and trust me, God never would give us more than we can bear.

Galatians 6:9 And let us not grow weary while doing good, for in due season we shall reap if we do not lose heart.

I love Jesus. In that beautiful song 'When I Survey the Wondrous Cross' in the last verse of the song, it says: 'Were the whole realm of nature mine, that were a present far too small. Love so amazing, so divine, demands my soul, my life my all.'

DIRECTION

I started to seek God for direction. So I went on a forty day fast. Like I said, fasting is a lifestyle for me. I just love it, and I do it with joy. The Lord told me during the fast that He had to allow things in my life to go the way they did, because He had a plan and purpose for my life. He said "Jean, I have blessed you with many dreams and visions. All these years I have been preparing you for ministry." The Lord said "I have called you to preach the gospel and you will start in your apartment, preaching to your own family." I heard these words from the Lord distinctly. I said "Lord, I will answer the call." I started to preach to my family. We had tambourines. We started church at 11 o'clock in the morning because we didn't want to wake up people.

Psalm 37:23 The steps of a good man are ordered by the LORD: and he delighteth in his way.

The Lord spoke to a woman in the Church where I got kicked out from and told her to leave that church and join us. And the Lord told her she must tithe by us also. Then the Lord added another family. So the apartment was getting crowded. We had church in the apartment for about 7 weeks. People started to go to the management to complain about us; that we were making too much noise. The office called me and when I went to the office, they said to me "Mrs. Tracey, the tenants are complaining of noise on Sunday mornings in your church services, and we are very sorry but you cannot have services in your apartment." They had a party room right in the building and I said to the lady in the office "Do you think they would rent me the party room for Sunday services and for Bible Study during the week?" I asked them what the cost would be. They told me they would have to take the matter to their board.

She told me I would have to write them a letter stating exactly what I want it for, and the days and times. I asked her, how long it would take her to get back to me. She said four days. She did and she said "Mrs. Tracey congratulations, they approved your letter." And she said I could only have 35 people in there. I said "Ok that is fine." I went on a 21 day fast just to give God praise and thanks. I bought one dozen roses and I gave them to the girl in the office - she was very happy. So church was no longer in my apartment. Church was now in the party room in the lobby. We had two services on Sundays, and it was really growing fast. We used to go out and witness, so it was really growing. We had bible study mid week. We had prayer meeting in our apartment with my family; we made sure we didn't pray too loud. One Sunday afternoon, I was preaching on the Baptism in the Holy Ghost, and seven people got filled. Praise God.

The next day people started to complain about the noise, and they called me to the office and said "We are very sorry but you can't have church in the party room." We will give you two weeks more. All in all we were there for about 7 to 8 weeks. So the girl told me they have a recreation room outside the building near the back. You had to go down some stairs. Near the recreation room was a convenience store, a pool, and a few other things.

She took me to see the room. It was very clean and it could seat 100 people inside. She said to me "You will have to write a letter and they will take it to the board." I wrote the letter and I started to fast. And I really cried out to God. I said "God beyond a shadow of a doubt I know you called me. Lord when I was in the church I did not presumptuously pick up myself and walk out, they kicked me out. And I know God because you alone know who I am inside out, I would not just walk out of the will of God and go and preach. You said you are ready for me to preach the gospel and Lord you have seen me go willingly. I have answered the call. I have started church in my apartment and they complained there is too much noise. I came down to the party room there is too much noise. Lord what is going on? God, I don't do anything in the flesh. I fast, I pray, I am in your word, Lord I wait on you every step of the way. Mighty God I do not understand all these hindrances. Please give me the grace and God's divine wisdom in all this, for my eyes are upon you Lord."

Psalm 46:1 God is our refuge and strength, a very present help in trouble.

Out of the blues just like a whirlwind God came in and He said to me "Jean every time satan comes in, and he would try to hinder the work, I will use it as a stepping stone. I will move you on to the next step. Know for sure my daughter I will never leave you nor forsake you, I will be with you to the very end for I have chosen you from your mother's womb, and no weapon formed against you will prosper: I am leading you to the next step, just follow me." After the Lord spoke to me, I started to really praise Him. I extended my fast another week only to give God praise and thanks.

The office called me up, and they said "Everything has been approved." We could now have service in the recreation room. This was outside the building; there was no one to complain there because we were outside. God is so good. This room could seat between 80 and 100 people. We bought equipment drums, keyboard, guitar and microphones etc. And God has been very good to us.

Psalm 38:4 O taste and see that the LORD is good: blessed is the man that trusteth in him.

The enemy attacks

My oldest son Gary got sick. At that time he was learning to drive. He had to go to classes because they had theory, and then they would take them out on the road.

When he left that morning, when the time came for him to come home, he didn't. Three or four hours past and he did not show up. I prayed and cried to God begging him to send my son home, or to let him call. This was very unusual; the kids are not like that. They know they have to call home if something is wrong. All of a sudden the phone rang, it was Gary. In a very faint voice, he said "Hi mom." I said "Are you feeling ok? Where are you?" He said "I am lying down in Eglinton subway station." I said "Why? Aren't you well?" Then he hung up.

Now I know for a fact that was not my son; it was the devil acting through him. I ran out of the house bare foot and got into the car and drove to Eglinton subway station. I searched the whole subway station and I was crying all the time and I was saying "God please let me find him." My search was in vain. I came back home, and I called the police. Three of them came. While I was talking to the police he walked in. The Lord brought him home. I gave him something to drink and we asked him to sit down because the police wanted to talk to him. When the police asked him what had happened and where he was he said he didn't know, he couldn't remember anything. When the police asked him how he got home, he said he took the bus. Let me get to the point. My son had a nervous breakdown. And this child would be so sick, and he would be in and out of the hospital. All this would be going on for the next two years.

This test was definitely to get me to stop preaching, this is all the devil wanted. But the devil is a liar and he is a loser. He can never win. Two long years; this was blood, sweat, and tears.

I started to fast and pray; this is my lifestyle. I don't know any other way, and this what I knew to do best. I took Gary to the doctor. And the doctor said "It is a nervous breakdown." He referred him to a psychiatrist and it is like the song writer wrote: "Onward Christian soldier, marching as to war."

I can honestly say going through this test two years seemed like eternity. But God gave me the grace and the strength every step of the way. Sometimes he would eat like a horse; he never stopped. There were other times you would have to beg him to eat. He would lie down and sleep a lot. He would read his bible if he was up to it. I used to beg him "Please read the word and please pray and ask God to help you." Sometimes you had to plead with him to take a bath, other times that would be the first thing he would do when he got up in the morning. There are times he would act up. I would have to take him to the hospital. They would admit him in the psychiatric ward and he would be in the hospital for five to seven weeks at a time. And this went on for two years.

One day he had a little bottle of poison in his hand and he locked his bedroom door. And I was calling him for his lunch, and he was carrying on loud, at the top of his voice, laughing, singing, shouting you name it. I stood by the door and I said "Son, please come and have your lunch." I begged him to open the door, and he said no. I don't know where he got the poison from to this day. I don't know. I knew my son was sick, I wouldn't have knives and stuff around, all these things were hidden from him. I would not have poison around like that. He said "If you keep bothering me I will drink the poison." I begged him, and said "Please don't drink it." I told him "I will call the police." He said "If you call the police I will drink it." I said "Please don't." He would not open his door. I stood right by the door, and I could hear every word he was saying.

I went to the phone, I spoke very quietly and I called the police. I told them about the poison and the police came. They begged him to open the door. One of the police said to him "Look how you have your mother crying to break her heart; please open the door." Finally he opened the door. The police took the poison from him and I gave him his dinner. He took his bath, and I prayed with him. I read a chapter from the word to him, and he went to sleep.

Every single day I prayed for him, anointed him with oil, and read the word for him. When there was church, he never put up a fight. He would shower, put on a suit, and go to church, and lie down in a corner on the floor from the beginning of the service to the very end. Very seldom would he sit up. I said very little to the congregation about him. I don't understand why, but very little was said. People would look at him lying on that cold floor throughout the service. I had to stand and preach that Jesus is a miracle worker while my son was very sick. I had to preach we must have faith in God and sometimes I felt like I didn't have any. I had to preach Jesus heals the broken hearted while I was bleeding inside. I had to preach Jesus heals the wounds, the hurt and the pains and in my heart I had all three. Sometimes I would sit and cry for hours and hours.

Revelation 2:10 Fear none of those things which thou shalt suffer: behold, the devil shall cast some of you into prison, that ye may be tried; and ye shall have tribulation ten days: be thou faithful unto death, and I will give thee a crown of life.

Gary would tell me all the time "Mom, I hate you. You have to stop preaching." He would be in front of the doctor and he would say "Mom I hate you." When I went to the hospital to see him when he was admitted I would take clean clothes for him to wear and I would cook food for him. I would bake cake and nice bread for him; everything I know he liked, I would make it for him. I would sit and see to it that he ate. No matter what I did, he would always tell me he hated me and I had to stop preaching.

The devil was after 2 things; he wanted me to quit preaching (satan was really after the ministry), and he wanted me to hate my son.

1 Peter 5:8 Be sober, be vigilant; because your adversary the devil, as a roaring lion, walketh about, seeking whom he may devour:

I always said to the devil, "I will not hate my child and I will not stop preaching. I will preach with all my heart in that pulpit" never mind the bleeding inside. I am the one who had to look after him while he was sick. His father had absolutely no patience with him. One day Gary was talking to me really rough, and his father got really angry at him and was going to hit him. I jumped right in the middle of them and I said to my husband, "Don't you dare touch him. Hit me if you want. But don't touch him." And my husband quieted down.

My kids did not speak to me anyhow; that is not the way I trained them, but I knew this was not the child. I knew this was satan working in him, and through him. The target was me and I recognized it from day one.

My fasted life, my prayer life and studying the word of God; I would not trade these three things for billions of dollars. I love the Lord Jesus with all my heart. My mother, my sister and my children would always tell me that under this sun they have never seen or heard about anyone like me. I would reply "It was only because of Jesus. He gets all the glory, the honor and the praise."

Revelation 4:11 Thou art worthy, O Lord, to receive glory and honor and power: for thou hast created all things, and for thy pleasure they are and were created.

There was a convention in Chicago, and I prayed about it, and God gave me the green light to go. I got my things packed and everything, I got up, took my shower, prayed, cooked, got dressed and ready for the airport. Gary started to act up. I recognized immediately it was the devil. I said satan "You don't want me to go to this conference, but in the name of Jesus, watch me." I called the ambulance, and I prayed with Gary. I sent him to the hospital. I called a cab and I went to the airport. I was about my Heavenly Father's business, and I knew God would take care of my son. In everything I do, God has to be first; I will have it no other way. I was bleeding inside for my son, but God must come before him. When I returned from my trip, I went to see him. In a couple of weeks he was discharged. One year was over, and he was still very sick. I decided I would go on a very long fast only for Gary and I would hear what God has to say. Towards the end of the fast this is what I received:

Isaiah 57:18-19 I have seen his ways, and will heal him: I will lead him also, and restore comforts unto him and to his mourners. I create the fruit of the lips; Peace, peace to him that is far off, and to him that is near, saith the LORD; and I will heal him.

I stood on these words, and I held God to it. These words meant more to me than gold and silver. Every single day, after I got these promises from God I would pray these words every day.

He would be in and out of the hospital, I was still preaching strong, and I had bible study to teach, and prayer meetings to carry on. I also had two services on Sundays, but God gave me the grace. I couldn't do it without Jesus. After two long years, God healed my son. The ministry started in 1988, Gary became sick that very year and two years later, God healed him. He got married in 1991, and he has four children. The devil fought this particular child so much. After he got married, he was into pornography. He would go to church on a Sunday, and later he would go to the strip joint. This was another episode. This went on and on. I would pray with him, and tried to show him the way out.

"God hates this sin" I told him all the time, "and this is not fair to your family." This was another test for me. The devil said to me "You have to quit ministry now. Look at your son." I said "Satan, in Jesus name, my son did not call me. God called me. And no matter what you do, God will give me the grace." God healed him from the pornography. All my children are married now, and I have 10 grandchildren; 6 granddaughters and 4 grandsons.

Exodus 15:26 And said, If thou wilt diligently hearken to the voice of the LORD thy God, and wilt do that which is right in his sight, and wilt give ear to his commandments, and keep all his statutes, I will put none of these diseases upon thee, which I have brought upon the Egyptians: for I am the LORD that healeth thee.

A DEMON

We were still in the recreation room and we used to witness in the neighborhood a lot. The church was growing, God moved in that room in a mighty way. We were there for a few years. One Sunday night a young girl was really acting up. This was my first experience with one that was possessed.

We had a visiting preacher and while the preacher was preaching, she started to manifest. (This was my very first encounter and I laughed until I got a headache). The devil was talking back to me. I said "Satan, in Jesus name, obey the servant of the most High God." The demon was really talking back. I said "Come out of her now in Jesus name." The demon said, "I am not coming out. I love her."

The visiting preacher started to pray for her and she gave him one slap in his face. I felt so bad. I asked the man to go. The children and I and some other sisters were there with the girl. I said to the demon "Why did you hit the preacher?" The demon said, "He is not living clean." I said to the demon, "Why didn't you hit me?" The demon replied, "You are a very Holy woman." I said "O.K. well come out of her in Jesus' name."

I didn't know much. I laughed and I laughed. I now know it wasn't funny. But it was something! She calmed down but the demons were still in her. The next day people reported me. They told the office as they were going to the convenience store that they heard this loud screaming going on in the church and that I was performing exorcisms. So they told me the church has to move. They didn't touch where I was living. But we couldn't have church there. This girl that was possessed took quite a while to be delivered but God set her free after a few months. Praise God; He is so Good.

Matthew 10:8 Heal the sick, cleanse the lepers, raise the dead, cast out devils: freely ye have received, freely give.

I started to pray and fast and I said "God we need a place and we need one fast. Please lead me Lord where to go next. There was a Radisson Hotel not far from where we had church. The Lord said "Go there." I met with them at the hotel and when they told me what

71

it would cost, I said "Lord, you would really have to bless me with a miracle each week." But God never failed, He always came in. God is so faithful.

Psalm 117:2 For his merciful kindness is great toward us: and the truth of the LORD endureth for ever. Praise ye the LORD.

We were there for one full year and God moved mightily in that hotel. This same demon possessed girl got her deliverance in that hotel; I held a crusade and she was completely delivered. God is so good. We had three meetings a week in the hotel; prayer meetings on Fridays, Bible Study on Wednesdays, and church service on Sundays.

THE CHURCH IN GUYANA

Since we were in the recreation centre, we started the project of building the church in Guyana where the Lord told me to build on my mother's land (the preacher had told me that God would not call a woman to build a church). It took a few years to build and it was huge. It could seat about 1,500 to 2,000 people easily. The missionary home also was built just next to the church. My mother (God bless her soul) gave me the land to build the church. God is an awesome God. The church and the missionary home was completed in 1995. I took 40 people down to Guyana (from Canada) for the opening of the church.

We had a great time in the Lord, we had invited a lot of people on the Island for the opening; the place was packed. So we do have a branch of this church in Canada, and in Guyana, South America where I was born. As soon as the church was opened, we stayed in Guyana for a week. Some people had to leave before, because they had to come back to go to work. After we left, we stopped in Trinidad for a few days. I preached in Trinidad, also. Then we came back to Canada.

My older sister preaches in the church in Guyana. She was saved long before me. Her husband died a few years ago, but she is really trying. God is mighty.

When we came back from the trip, all hell broke loose. A few families that went on the trip with me started to leave the church. The devil deceived these people, it was so sad. I missed these people so much because we all were very close. I loved them so much. I took this on, one full year. But God brought me through. I thank God for all the different experiences He has allowed me to go through in ministry, because every one of them drew me closer to God and trust me, I have learned a lot. God is God. He says in His word

Matthew 16:18 And I say also unto thee, That thou art Peter, and upon this rock I will build my church; and the gates of hell shall not prevail against it.

Maybe the devil thought I would quit, but satan had the wrong person.

ORDINATION

The Lord made a way and I was ordained. This was a huge miracle. What a Saviour. Then after a while my two sons were ordained, Pastor Gary Tracey and Pastor Bruce Tracey. Now, I have two sons, who are assistant pastors. Jesus is Lord. Praise Him.

Psalm 100:2 Serve the LORD with gladness; Come before His presence with singing.

We moved out of the hotel, because we were there one full year and the Lord spoke to me to call up a preacher we knew. I asked him if we could share their building with them. The preacher set up an appointment for me to go in to see the place and to meet him and his wife so we could discuss certain things. This preacher and his wife were very nice people who love the Lord. When their Service on Sunday ended, we would have our service. We had prayer meeting during the week, and also bible study. Everything worked out well. Praise the Lord - that pastor and his church were very good to us.

THE CALL

Something very profound took place while we had church there. The call of God upon my life is to "Prepare the End Time Bride." The Lord told me that from the time He called me to preach. It was quite something. When He told me that, I said "Lord, that is the call for every preacher." That is what every preacher is supposed to be doing; souls coming in and getting saved, the preacher preparing the church for the rapture, preaching the Word of God uncompromised, and in fear and trembling. The Lord said to me "Not so Jean, not everyone that stands in the pulpit was called by me, and was sent. Many in the pulpits went. I did not send them." I said "O.k. Lord." The Lord told me many of them are hirelings, and the Lord said also to me. "Even the ones I did call and send, even they are messing up big time." I said "Lord, please keep me faithful to the end. Bless me with a shepherd's heart and keep me pure."

1 Jude 24-25 Now unto him that is able to keep you from falling, and to present you faultless before the presence of his glory with exceeding joy, To the only wise God our Saviour, be glory and majesty, dominion and power, both now and ever. Amen.

The Lord said to me "Jean I want you to dress as a bride." I was to preach the message dressed as a bride for that Sunday service. I had to wear a bridal gown, crown and veil, gloves and everything like a bride. I said "Lord, these people are going to think I am nuts." I said to the Lord I will do it but I would like 3 confirmations before I open my mouth to the church or to my family. I never said a word to anyone. In that same week the Lord started to confirm what He said. A lady in the church brought me a lamp for my night table. This lamp was a bride; a bride fully dressed in a bridal outfit, and very beautiful. This was the first confirmation.

In that same week someone else came to me. She is a very godly woman. She said to me "Pastor Jean, I dreamt you were walking down the aisle fully dressed as a bride, and you were alone with no bridegroom." This was the second confirmation. Someone else the following week came to me and said "Pastor Jean I had a dream about you. You had on a beautiful wedding gown fully dressed like a bride and you were preaching." This was the third confirmation.

I said to the Lord, "I am so sorry dear God, but I need two more." In the following week someone came to me in the church and said to me "Pastor Jean I saw you dressed as a bride and you looked so beautiful." In the same week, another person came to me. This person was very young. She said to me "Pastor Jean, I dreamt you dressed as a bride and I was fixing your trail." This was the fifth confirmation.

So within three weeks I had five confirmations. I obeyed God and I wore this Bridal gown. I borrowed it from my daughter; the crown, the veil, the gloves and everything. Of course, there were a few people who thought I was losing it, or I had lost it; but I was completely sound. I told the congregation about it, after I received all the confirmations. I asked them to really pray for me. I got specific instructions from God for that service. Oh the presence of God was so strong in that service. It was quite something; I made sure I carried out all the instructions from God to the letter. Glory to God in the Highest. Jesus is coming for His bride, without spot, or wrinkle, or without blemish. Not one sin can enter into Heaven.

Revelation 21:27 And there shall in no wise enter into it any thing that defileth, neither whatsoever worketh abomination, or maketh a lie: but they which are written in the Lamb's book of life.

I will never forget that day. It was quite something.

Go West

We had to move from there, because the place was packed. We couldn't fit more people. So we had to move. I started to pray and fast for direction. The Lord said "Go west." I said "God if I am to go west to preach, and if the church has to go west, intervene supernaturally, so that I can know this is what you are saying. Allow me, Lord, to get a phone call from someone. Let it be about west and church related." I fasted and I prayed. Anything I have to do I have to seek God. Never ever try to do things in the flesh. You will get in a lot of trouble with God. One day I was really crying out to God. Anytime I am praying I turn off the ringer on the phone. Even if it rings, you can't hear it. I like to pray undisturbed. I would make sure I cooked and everything before I went into prayer, so no one could say that they are hungry. As children of God, we must live a very blameless life.

Proverbs 11:20 They that are of a froward heart are abomination to the LORD: but such as are upright in their way are his delight.

When I was finished praying, I turned up the phone, and it rang an hour later. I knew a woman who has a church in the west end. We talked occasionally. This lady was really crying on the phone, so I said "Pastor, are you ok? Do you feel sick or anything? Please tell me and I will pray for you." She cried and cried. She said "Pastor Jean, I have some bad news. The land lord just boarded up the church." "You could not pay the rent?" I asked. I told her, "Let us pray." After praying, I asked "Can we go to coffee? Which day are you available?"

I took the secretary and we picked her up. Everywhere I go I take someone with me. I do not go out by myself. We met for coffee and she told me the whole story. She said "The people hardly pay their tithes," and so many other things were not going too well. She said "I was carrying a lease, and my time was not up yet, but it is up now, because I did not pay about six months rent, they boarded up the place. Do you know of any preacher that may want to rent the place? It wouldn't look too bad on me. If somebody good comes up I will take them to the landlord myself. Do you know anyone?" I said to her "This is an answer to prayer. I will take the place." She took me to her land lord right away.

Up to this day, the man never asked me for a reference or anything. All he said was "Yes, you can have the place right away." I knew it was God. Again God moved mightily in that place, while we were there.

The people remained faithful (the ones who lived in the east) like myself and my family. They drove way down there for church. Faithfulness and commitment to God are so important. Once God places you in a church, distance must not be a problem. By this time in the ministry, I knew a little more about casting out demons, and praying that God will deliver them. A lot of people were delivered and set free by the power of the Holy Spirit. The anointing and the power of God was at work in that place. We remained faithful, regardless of the distance; many came in and got saved, healed and delivered.

John 8:32 And ye shall know the truth, and the truth shall make you free.

1997

On our way to church there is a mall that we would have to pass while driving. You can see it from the highway. I did not drive that day, my daughter-in-law did. I was sitting in the back seat with her kids. As we drove by Yorkdale mall a voice said to me "Jean, look on the right." When I looked I saw a very bright light flashing these figures "1997." I saw this sometime in 1996. These figures were just flashing, I saw this three times. I never said anything. I remained very quiet and I pondered this whole thing. What I had there was an open vision. Most of the times once I am around people, even my own family, I like to be very quiet. I don't talk if I don't have to. I never like gossip, I don't like vain talk, I always like to be very quiet.

1 Timothy 2:1-3 I exhort therefore, that, first of all, supplications, prayers, intercessions, and giving of thanks, be made for all men; For kings, and for all that are in authority; that we may lead a quiet and peaceable life in all godliness and honesty. For this is good and acceptable in the sight of God our Saviour;

1 Thessalonians 4:11 And that ye study to be quiet, and to do your own business, and to work with your own hands, as we commanded you;

Isaiah 30:15 For thus saith the Lord GOD, the Holy One of Israel; In returning and rest shall ye be saved; in quietness and in confidence shall be your strength: and ye would not.

So I pondered this thing and I said "Lord what will take place in 1997?" Two Sundays after this vision, I felt led of the Lord to share it with the church, and I did. Praise God. Oh I love Jesus so much. He is so faithful. I started to fast immediately after I received this vision, and I asked "God what about 1997? What are you saying to me?" He said "I will bless you with your own church. You will not have to rent." I said "O.k. Lord, but we don't have a dime in the bank." The Lord said "Jean, don't I know that? You will have this church in the east end. So that means you will have to go back east." I said, "Lord, wherever you lead me, I will follow." As the song says: "Where he leads me, I will follow. Where He leads me, I will follow. Where He leads me, I will follow. I'll go with Him, with Him all the way."

80

The enemy in the church

Because God was moving so mightily there, of course satan sent a witch to destroy me and the church. I can honestly say that God has blessed me with a gift, and that gift is the spirit of discernment. Every preacher on the face of this earth needs this gift. She was in the church for almost one full year. From the day she walked in I knew she was a witch. Satan has his people in every church. If the pulpit doesn't have a spirit of discernment, they will mash up your whole church. The devil will assign his people to destroy the church. Once the discernment is there you will pray "But God said I will build my church and the gates of hell will not come against it."

Satan sends his people to sow discord among the brethren, she would cast spells on the congregation. She would sit there and chant in the services; she kept chanting and all the little children would start to cry. We didn't have a nursery, there was no room there for a nursery. They would try to do their gymnastics so people would leave the church. When these witches and warlocks are in the church, weak Christians suffer a lot. I always let the church know that if they live in sin, there is an opening for satan to come in. I've always taught the flock, pray every single day, study the word of God every single day. If you don't do these things, you have nothing to keep you. I hate satan with a passion, and with every fiber of my being. This devil is a liar; he came to steal, kill and destroy. Jesus said He came that we might have life, and have it more abundantly.

John 10:10 The thief cometh not, but for to steal, and to kill, and to destroy: I am come that they might have life, and that they might have it more abundantly.

This witch would come in and sit in the front seat. I would always observe her. When the saints of God are dancing in the Spirit, she is right there, dancing, you name it. I prayed and prayed. I alerted all the elders and all the ushers. We have women ushers and men ushers. The Lord showed me one day that she likes the washrooms and she loves mirrors. I don't know why she would chant in front of the mirrors. So I wrote on the top of the mirrors in the washrooms 'Satan, the blood of Jesus is against you.' She tried desperately to destroy me and all the church. All I see is this woman's soul. One elder said to me one day "Kick her out." I said "No, I can't do that. I was kicked out of a church and I would not want my enemy to go through that. But if God tells me to do it, I will."

Luke 6:27 But I say unto you which hear, Love your enemies, do good to them which hate you,

We prayed for her soul to be saved all the time. But, when you looked at her, she was getting worse. She would greet me like everybody else. Satan is very bold. You may ask "Why does God allow these things in the church?" I believe this was a big test for me. I was very concerned about the baby Christians, also I was concerned about the back-slidden ones. But I put them under the blood night and day. That is all I can do. I prayed and asked God to keep them. The devil brings in his people all the time just like he did with her. But God will prevail always. After a while, I started to pray and ask God to move her out if she will not repent. I fasted and prayed and I really cried out. After 9 long months the Lord spoke to me. The Lord said "Jean, have the elders bring her to the office, sit and have a talk with her." The Lord said "She has had enough chances to repent, but she would not." I said "Lord, in this meeting, what do I say to her?" The Lord said "I will give you the words in that hour."

The service started. The elders were watching for her, when she came in, so they could tell her that the Pastor would like to see her for a few minutes. But none of this ever happened. She never came back that Sunday or ever. The devil is such a liar. No matter what he tries to do, God will protect His own. We have had witches come in to destroy the work of God. Just as they come in, they leave. But this one was daring, I was never afraid, because God has not given me a spirit of fear.

1 John 4:4 Ye are of God, little children, and have overcome them: because greater is he that is in you, than he that is in the world.

I know who I am in Christ. I know my walk, I know my talk, and I know my life. Nothing under this sun satan tries to do can ever touch me. I am under the blood, and I will stay under the blood.

Repent

I have seen when Christians open themselves to satan and live in sin and practice sin. They are the most miserable people on the face of this earth. Preachers preach that a Christian can never be demon possessed. I believe this with all my heart. But we do not stop there. We must tell the people. If a Christian practices sin, they can be possessed. If they don't want to repent genuinely, and turn from that sin, that sin has them captive, they don't have control over that sin. The Bible teaches us:

Romans 6:14 For sin shall not have dominion over you: for ye are not under the law, but under grace.

But today we don't want to call sin what it is. We just want to say, "Ok they have some struggles, but they are practicing sin." They are not only possessed, but they are possessed with legions. The devil is a liar. They need deliverance just like any sinner out there.

2 Corinthians 5 Examine yourselves, whether ye be in the faith; prove your own selves. Know ye not your own selves, how that Jesus Christ is in you, except ye be reprobates?

If we are going to live like the sinner, something is drastically wrong. Now for that child of God to really come back to God once they have fallen away, it would not be easy. For the word of God says:

Hebrews 6:4-8 For it is impossible for those who were once enlightened, and have tasted the heavenly gift, and have become partakers of the Holy Spirit, and have tasted the good word of God and the powers of the age to come, if they fall away, to renew them again to repentance, since they crucify again for themselves the Son of God, and put Him to an open shame. For the earth which drinks in the rain that often comes upon it, and bears herbs useful for those by whom it is cultivated, receives blessing from God; but if it bears thorns and briers, it is rejected and near to being cursed, whose end is to be burned

Proverbs 13:15 Good understanding giveth favour, but the way of transgressors is hard.

The churches are filled with witches and satanists. If the pulpit is not living and walking pure, if they don't have discernment, if they are not praying and fasting, if they are sick spiritually because of sin, then the whole church is sick. God is calling us to repentance. I say us because I am always the least. There is a wake up call. Whoever has ears to hear, will hear that call. The Lord is good.

ANOTHER MOVE

The Lord said "It is time now to buy a place of our own." I said "Lord we don't have any money to put as a down payment for a place." The Lord said "Jean, you just obey me."

I said "Lord, send me the right person, send all the right people, whoever and whatever, just lead me every step of the way." I went to the congregation. I said "Thus saith the Lord; we have to purchase a building and let us cry out to God in prayer and fasting."

I met a woman, a real estate agent, a Christian. I said to her "We need a place, but the Lord says we have to go east. Right now we have a church in the west end, but God wants us to buy a place in the east end. My family and I live in the east end anyways." So this is good for us. She said "So what will the price range be?" I said to her "$1.5 million, but we don't have a dime." This woman thought I was nuts. She laughed and laughed. So I said to her, "Once God says it, He will do it. God must know we don't have a dime. God knows it all. But we just have to trust Him, and take one day at a time. God will lead every step of the way." She said Pastor Jean, "I have never seen anyone like you." I said it is not me, it is God.

1 Corinthians 15:41 There is one glory of the sun, and another glory of the moon, and another glory of the stars: for one star differeth from another star in glory.

She found a place that was listed in that same price range. So she asked me to set up an appointment with her to go and see the place. This place sits on 2 acres of land. It was a church, another congregation was there and they wanted to sell. It had pews and everything, it was nice. I took my family and the elders to see this place - everybody liked it. It had a huge kitchen but there was a lot of work to be done on it. We prayed and we fasted, we cried out to God. "Lord, is this the place you have for us?" The Lord said "This is the place." I called the agent after a few days. I said "I believe this is the building God wants us to have, and so shall it be, in Jesus name." Every time I talked to this woman, she would laugh.

I went to the bank, and I said to the loan officer "You will find my story a very strange one, however, let me introduce myself." After the introduction I said "I am a minister, and would like to purchase a building for the Church." He asked me what the cost was and I told him about $1.5 million, and that I needed a mortgage. He asked how much I had to put down. I said "Not a dime." He asked "So what are you doing here?" I replied, "I came so you could help me. Tell me what I need to do." He said, "If you can raise $500,000 you will get the mortgage. Do you think you can raise that?" I said, "I can't but God will help me. How long do I have?" "Come back to see me in seven days," he replied. "Sir, I thank you for your time. I will be here in seven days."

For 7 days I cried out to God by day and by night. People in the church were also fasting and praying; the elders and the ushers. Everybody was praying. I asked the congregation to believe God with me that we can raise the $500,000. The people responded well. I said "God, I cannot do anything by myself, I am helpless. But God I can do all things through Christ who strengthens me." I said to the church, "Some of you may have to take out a loan; some of you may have to get a second mortgage on your home, whatever it takes, let us all join together and do what we have to do in Jesus' name." Faith is great, but faith without works is dead.

James 2:18 Yea, a man may say, Thou hast faith, and I have works: shew me thy faith without thy works, and I will shew thee my faith by my works.

I did go back to the bank in seven days. I said to the loan officer "You carry on, all things are in the hands of God." By faith I believe God will come through. This man looked at me as though I was crazy. So I said "You do what you have to do, and I will do what I have to do." He said "What do you have to do?" I said "I will stay on my knees." I witnessed to this man. I said to him "It is only Jesus." He said to me "I have never met someone like you. You are an amazing woman." I said to him, "I am nothing without Jesus. It is only the Lord."

I told him about the Lord. He listened intently. Many times I would see the tears settle in his eyes. I said "Thank you sir, God richly bless you."

We had to come up with the $500,000 in less than one month, and seven days were already gone. We had three weeks left, and still we didn't have a dime. I know beyond a shadow of a doubt God would not fail me. The Lord is so good. Everybody started to work on getting their money together. The church prayed, and prayed. We all came together in unity, as one body asking God with one voice for this. May I say we had a few doubting Thomases; just a few – but our eyes were on Jesus.

Hebrews 3:1 Wherefore, holy brethren, partakers of the heavenly calling, consider the Apostle and High Priest of our profession, Christ Jesus;

Keep your Eyes on Jesus

The one thing I focused on was the vision God gave me on the highway at Yorkdale Mall, when I saw 1997 flashing three times. The Lord did say we were going to move into our own place in 1997. I didn't mind the doubting Thomases; in everything you will have them. They were there in Jesus' day and they are there today. What matters is what you do about it. I always kept my eyes on Jesus. The minute you take your eyes off Christ you will start to sink (see Matthew 14:24-33). In this story the storm was raging, and the ship was tossed to and fro with the waves. Then Jesus appeared to the disciples walking on the water, going towards them. Peter said to Jesus, Lord bid me to come to you on the water. Peter got out of the ship and started to walk on the water towards Jesus. But when Peter saw the wind and waves were boisterous, he was afraid and he began to sink and he cried out "Lord save me." And Jesus stretched out his hands and caught him.

No matter what you have to face in life as a child of God, keep your eyes on Jesus. If you take your eyes off Him you will start to sink. Jesus gives us the victory all the time, not in our way or in our time. He does it in His way and in His time. Praise the Lord.

Psalm 27:14 Wait on the LORD: be of good courage, and he shall strengthen thine heart: wait, I say, on the LORD.

The deal was closing the last Friday in April 1997 at 12 noon. In 3 days time we had to move into our building. We had to move in on the 1st of May 1997. What a Saviour. When the deal was going to close at 12 o'clock that day, up to 11 o'clock that very day we still needed $150,000. I got up early that morning and I had my shower, and I prayed. I was fasting, of course. That was a must. I prayed and prayed and there were others (the brethren) praying. When I was finished praying, I made a cup of coffee and sat by the phone from 7 a.m. that morning. I anointed my phone with oil. I said "God, this $150,000 has to be met in Jesus name. And Lord, the saints of God are going to call and say they got their loans from the bank and whatever, whoever, however. God, the Holy Ghost is coming in with every dime."

Psalm 121:2 My help cometh from the LORD, which made heaven and earth.

Calls started to come in from the saints from the north, the south, the east and the west. "Pastor Jean I got through, I am bringing $10,000." Another call came in "Pastor Jean, I got $15,000" and the calls kept pouring in. At 10 a.m. my son walked in, and he said "Mom, I am going to the bank for a loan, you pray." I prayed with him, he went to the bank, got through very fast, and he returned with $30,000. We needed $25,000 before 12 noon and it was about 11:30 a.m. We just had ½ an hour more to go. I started to get dressed to leave home for the bank. The secretary phoned and she said "I will meet you at the bank with the rest of the money." People had phoned her to pick up their money. Glory to God in the Highest. All the money came in. The loans officer said "Congratulations." The loans officer did accept Jesus as his Lord and personal Saviour and when he did he was weeping so much. What a faithful Jesus. He is Lord.

We got the keys. I signed the paperwork. Oh what a mighty God we serve. We moved in the new place. We did a lot in that place. We carpeted the whole church. The men in the church, along with my family made offices, a nursery, you name it. The building was huge and the land was 2 acres. The place was nice. When we moved in we sanctified the whole building and the land; it took bottles upon bottles of olive oil. Then once the carpeting and all renovations were done, we had the opening. We invited a lot of people; including lots of preachers. The opening was great.

Proverbs 16:3 Commit thy works unto the LORD, and thy thoughts shall be established.

PERSECUTION

Then persecution started coming; one issue after the next. My eldest son and his family left the church. This was quite something. I do not blame his wife for anything. He was supposed to be the head of his house, and he should have taken that stand. He was away with his family for two long years. I cried and cried. Then he came back. He came back alone. God is good.

When my son left with his family, other people in the church left also, because of so many things, all kinds of lies, you name it; lots of people left. People would call the government and give all kinds of false reports. The auditors came in. We gave them all they asked for, and the government took away our charitable status. But I never gave up. People in the church couldn't have a receipt for their giving, so many left. The Lord said to me one day in prayer and fasting "I will destroy them that want to destroy you." But I always prayed to God for mercy for them. But the word of God says:

Romans 9:13-15 As it is written Jacob have I loved, but Esau I have hated. What shall we then? Is there unrighteousness with God? God forbid. For he saith to Moses, I will have mercy on whom I will have mercy and I will have compassion on whom I will have compassion.

The churches have the biggest hypocrites and this is so sad. They told so many lies about me. I always hung on to this scripture:

Acts 5:38-39 And now I say unto you, Refrain from these men, and let them alone: for if this counsel or this work be of men, it will come to nought: But if it be of God, ye cannot overthrow it; lest haply ye be found even to fight against God.

Man did not call me, God did. If I went, and I wasn't sent by God, trust me, I would already be dead, and there would be no Lord's church. (This is the name of our church; The Lord's Church.)

I do not interfere with people. I serve God in fear and trembling. I am never envious of people. Yet there is so much envy. So many witches come in. Just as they come in, they have to go. The battle is not mine, it is the Lord's. Jesus is fighting for me. I give God praise and thanks for the faithful few. God has really blessed me with some faithful people. I know God will bless them in return. These people to this day are really standing strong with me.

Ecclesiastes 12:13 Let us hear the conclusion of the whole matter: Fear God, and keep his commandments: for this is the whole duty of man.

The mortgage was getting very difficult to pay because a lot of the people who used to pay tithes left. I always had to borrow money to pay the mortgage. I prayed and fasted and asked the Lord for direction. The Lord told me to sell the building, so I did. Then we had to move. The Lord led us to a hotel. We were there for five years. God really moved in that hotel. When we had our own building God moved mightily there also. The tests continued one after the other. When we were in that hotel I could remember the Lord said to me I must go to the hotel for three days. Many times I would go away to a hotel for three or four days to fast and pray. However the Lord would lead me.

This particular weekend the Lord wanted me to go for three days. I packed and I got myself ready. My daughter had borrowed my vehicle to go on an errand. I was waiting on her to return so I could drive to the hotel. While I was waiting the phone rang. It was the police. He said to me, "Your daughter just had an accident; your vehicle is a total write off. The ambulance is here and they will take her to the hospital."

I called my son and I asked him to go with her. Someone called her husband at work, and he came down. The accident occurred on the opposite side of the street from where we had to make a left turn on to, in order to go to the hotel. If you made a right turn on that street two or three blocks down was the accident, and if you made a left turn on the street, you were heading towards the hotel.

I said to my husband "The devil is a liar. Now that I don't have a vehicle, please give me a ride to the hotel in your vehicle." My husband knows me well. He said, "You are going straight to the hotel, if I know you well." I said "Yes, please turn left. God will take care of my daughter and she will be just fine. I am going about my Father's business." So that morning my daughter was heading for the hospital in an ambulance, and I was heading for the hotel to pray and fast.

Deuteronomy 5:6 And thou shalt love the LORD thy God with all thine heart, and with all thy soul, and with all thy might.

When I got to the hotel, my husband dropped me off and went back home. I checked in, went up to my room, got out my bottle of oil, sanctified the whole room, chased out every demon, and invited God's presence into that hotel room. This is something I always do.

I started to cry out to my God "I am here on your business, and my daughter had an accident and she is at the hospital. God you are first in my life and this has always been. I ask you Lord, please heal my daughter, and she will go home."

Mark 12:29-31 And Jesus answered him, The first of all the commandments is, Hear, O Israel; The Lord our God is one Lord: And thou shalt love the Lord thy God with all thy heart, and with all thy soul, and with all thy mind, and with all thy strength: this is the first commandment. And the second is like, namely this, Thou shalt love thy neighbour as thyself. There is none other commandment greater than these.

I prayed and prayed. I called my daughter three or four hours after I prayed and she answered her cell phone. Her and her husband were just getting into their car to go home from the hospital. I said to my daughter "I am so sorry, but I am positive you understand." She replied "Yes mom, I do understand. Don't worry mom, I am fine." God is so good. That was Friday, and I said to her, I will see you on Sunday (I went to the hotel for three days to fast and pray). God must be first in everything. This was a giant test for me but I chose the Lord ahead of my daughter. Oh how I love Jesus. God visited me in that hotel in a powerful way, and he took care of my daughter. Praise God.

Luke 14:26 If any *man* come to me, and hate not his father, and mother, and wife, and children, and brethren, and sisters, yea, and his own life also, he cannot be my disciple.

Another Move

We were at the hotel for five years and the Lord spoke. He said we are to rent a place, and He would lead me where. He did. We left the hotel and presently we are renting a place not far away from the hotel. God is good and He is really moving. We are trusting God now for revival. The heat is still on. I know this will always be until Jesus comes. I love God now more than ever. We just moved in May 2008. God has great things in store for his universal church. Jesus is coming very soon, and we must be ready.

Luke 12:40 Be ye therefore ready also: for the Son of man cometh at an hour when ye think not.

My family

My husband and my four children and their families are all trying their best to serve the Lord, except for one member in my family (not my immediate family). This person is sold out to the devil, and cannot get more wicked and evil. I cannot say 'he' or 'she' for personal reasons. This is my thorn. But like God said to Paul, (the same words He said to me):

2 Corinthians 12:9 And he said unto me, My grace is sufficient for thee: for my strength is made perfect in weakness. Most gladly therefore will I rather glory in my infirmities, that the power of Christ may rest upon me.

One of my very own. Jesus said:

Matthew 10:35-36 For I am come to set a man at variance against his father, and the daughter against her mother, and the daughter in law against her mother in law. And a man's foes shall be they of his own household.

They want to destroy me and the church. But God sees it all. And God will do what He has to do. All I can do is pray. But beyond a shadow of a doubt I will pass this test in Jesus name.

I will glory in the cross. For me to live is Christ and to die is gain.

If this book has blessed your heart and if you do not know Jesus as your Lord and your Saviour, you can accept Him right now into your heart and life. Pray this prayer, and mean it:

Dear Lord Jesus, please forgive me of all my sins. I do repent Lord. Have mercy upon me. I now invite Jesus into my heart, as my Lord and Saviour. I believe you died on the cross and you rose from the dead. Thank you Lord for dying for my sins. Thank you Lord, for saving my soul. In Jesus name, Amen and Amen.

Romans 10:9-10 That if thou shalt confess with thy mouth the Lord Jesus, and shalt believe in thine heart that God hath raised him from the dead, thou shalt be saved. For with the heart man believeth unto righteousness; and with the mouth confession is made unto salvation.

A Message to the Backslider

You say "It is very hard. I can't handle the suffering. It is too much." Get back in the race quickly. God will give you the grace. He is married to the backslider.

Pray this prayer:
Precious Jesus, I have been running from you. I have been playing church. I do repent Lord. Have mercy on me, and please give me one more chance. I know without holiness I can never see your face. And Lord, I want to make heaven. Please forgive me Lord. I do repent.
In Jesus name,
Amen and Amen.

Acts 3:19 Repent ye therefore, and be converted, that your sins may be blotted out, when the times of refreshing shall come from the presence of the Lord.

Hebrews 12:14 Follow peace with all men, and holiness, without which no man shall see the Lord: